Nureyev

Valeria Crippa and Ralph Fassey

Nureyev

RIZZOLI
NEW YORK

Art director
Marcello Francone

Editorial coordination
Caterina Giavotto

Design
Antonietta Pietrobon

Translation
Judith Goodman

Photographs: © Ralph Fassey

First published in the United States of America in 2003 by
Rizzoli International Publications, Inc.
300 Park Avenue South
New York, NY 10010
www.rizzoliusa.com

© 2003 by Rizzoli libri illustrati
Società Editoria Artistica SpA
Gruppo Skira
www.skira.net

Library of Congress Control Number: 2003108821

ISBN: 0-8478-2544-2

Printed in Italy

Contents

Nureyev

by Valeria Crippa

Rudolf, So Near, So Far

The great photographer Robert Capa used to say that if a photograph is not good enough it is because it was not taken close enough. Photographing Nureyev, in words and images, means having had the privilege of being introduced into the exclusive world of the Flying Tartar. To be allowed to go behind the scenes, meet the people to whom he gave the few moments of his life that were not completely dedicated to the stage. It was a motley court that moved around a miraculous man. Furiously and tenaciously he would insist every single day that the dance was supreme among the arts, that the dance was more important than life itself. Entering into this world crowded with friends, fans, and VIPs, meant giving some part of oneself to that world.

It meant believing that work and art are the only and ultimate reasons for living. Nureyev had an extraordinary talent for looking into people. He had antenna that could catch the degree of passion in others. He used to say, "There is an invisible thread that connects people and unites them either for a few hours or for life."

This invisible thread was responsible for my chance meeting with Ralph Fassey. His wonderful cache of unpublished photographs had been hidden away, like buried treasure, in a drawer for twenty-five years.

In Fassey's photographs, Nureyev is caught at his apogee. He is suspended in an ideal of aesthetic perfection, in moments stolen from the tyranny of passing time. This is just as we want to remember him and how he is preserved in the collective imagination. Like all the stars that myths have made eternal, Nureyev has stayed like this, always young and shining.

Many biographies appeared all over the world after his death. Some were more detailed than others. This book is not intended as another objectively compiled biographical profile. It is, rather, the subjective narration of a great star, seen up close, behind the scenes, in his private moments, and human and vulnerable. It is told through a series of moments caught by a friendly lens. It retraces his life and appears on a stage that is as great as the world.

In the connection between dance and life, the line that in Nureyev separated reality from the fiction of the stage was as thin as tissue paper. Perhaps it would be better to say that it was as thin as a stage wing that allowed a glimpse of the characters that Nureyev played every evening in a different disguise. He removed them from the sugary iconography of the fable and transformed them into pulsating creatures through a catharsis of energy, blood, tears, and sweat.

"Rudolf, there's news from London . . . it seems that Margot is dying . . ." Pause. "Has she died?" "No, not yet. But this is the end." Silence. And then, in a quiet voice, concentrated in the stifled collapse into pain, "Thank you." I had to do this too. I would never have chosen to make that telephone call. In February 1991 Margot Fonteyn was in hospital in Panama. Nureyev kept in close touch from wherever his travels took him during a tour in the United States with his Friends. These were a small group of "friends" from the dance who were gathered together from time to time to give a performance. It was my fate to tell him. Included into a conversation about the usual banal daily details of work, I was deeply embarrassed to have to tell him that the greatest artistic dance partnership of the twentieth century had come to a close. It was really at an end.

Right to the last, Nureyev and Fonteyn had been bound together in a crystalline friendship. When Fonteyn was near, Nureyev's voice would change. It would be gentle, full of tenderness and memories. Over twenty-eight years, life had copied the theatre. In 1963 they performed at the Royal Opera House in the ballet *Marguerite and Armand* in front of a deliriously happy public. The choreographer, Frederick Ashton called it an *evocation poétique.* "Marguerite and Armand" continued away from the footlights: Nureyev/Armand kneeling in front of Fonteyn/Marguerite. He looks at her pale body, made bloodless by the illness, and he gives her the last salute by making the sign of the Cross. Then, as in the rules of pantomime, of which the English are masters, he follows her departing soul with a gesture of a hand toward the infinite. I heard later that after Nureyev received the news he shut himself in his room at the hotel and would not even open for the Friends. Pain is a private act.

One day Nureyev told me, "My meeting with Margot was a benediction. It was an encounter between two talents who spoke of the same things with the same passion. Destiny gave us a complementary talent, one integrated and completed the other. Margot used to say, 'I don't know what it is, but look at the photographs taken during our performances. We are always looking in the same direction. Our arms are in the same direction. It's a total purpose of movement.' Margot used to say that she loved dancing with me. I was strong, tumultuous. I jumped higher than the others and she

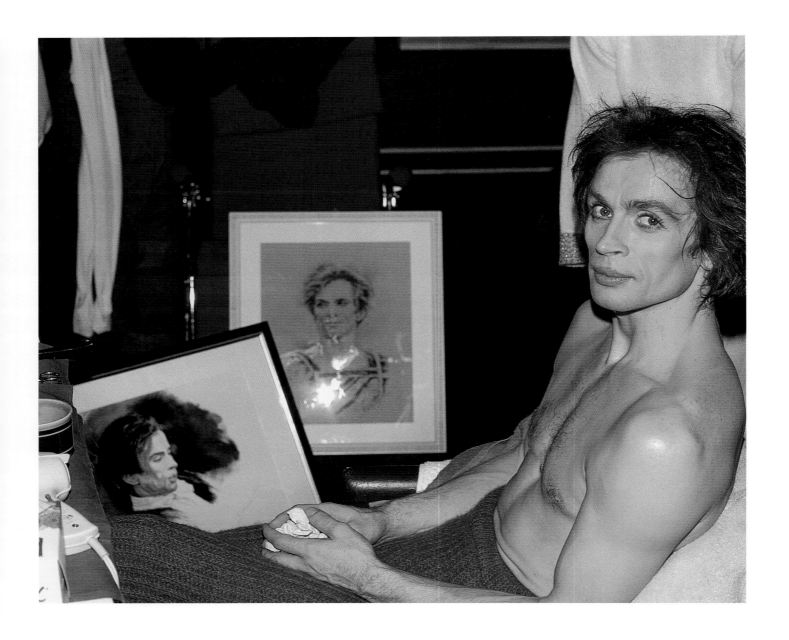

had to compete. It forced her to make choices that she would not have dared to make on her own. Ashton was very jealous of this. He even reproached her for listening more to me than to him. Nureyev and Fonteyn danced for the last time in *Mantova Festa a Corte*. They danced with Carla Fracci, exchanging baroque steps in a performance for RAI (Radio Televisione Italiana). The *pas de trois* had been choreographed by Francine Lancelot, the expert whom Nureyev hired at the Opéra de Paris when he was ballet director there.

To work for Nureyev was a great and exciting adventure. It was a theatre inside a theatre, a private and substantial place that refracted the great illusions of the stage. Nureyev knew how to create an electric quality of time. It tended to accelerate the lives of everybody around. It was a convulsive whisking up of events. He detested slackness in others. He would often talk laconically on the phone. Sometimes he was even cryptic. He would launch suspended nouns into the conversation, without offering any explanation to support them. He would do this to his ballerinas, often moving them with only one hand. He expected constant ready reflexes, open minds trained to catch any possible change in the conversation. It was like a game of multiple choice. Otherwise he would become irritated, and disappear from the other end of the line. Maybe this was because he tacitly appreciated the fact that from the very beginning of the phone call I would recognize his voice as he spoke my name. "Valeria . . ." "Yes, Rudolf." Once, on the telephone, I tried a more formal approach. "Rudolf, I hope I am not disturbing you . . ." His abrupt reply was "Why?" Of course, why? When it was about work, there were no excuses and no obstacles. He always arrived first. Even if he was on one of his very rare vacations, possibly on the rocks at his beloved Li Galli, the telephone would ring. There would be an immediate passing of the word among his Sorrentino workers. The message would be handed from one to another and he would climb up to get to the phone, leaving you waiting for minutes on end. It was certainly not a form of rigidly excessive zeal. It was not only professionalism. It was his way of living the dance and for the dance. This was a categorical imperative that you had to understand immediately if you wanted to be with him.

Rigor was one of the "Nureyev laws." The severity that he demanded of himself he also expected from others, starting with his partners (who were often mistreated), to the theatrical staff and whoever else contributed his work to the good outcome of the production.

He would usually speak in English. It was an English mixed with Russian overtones. In person, he would sometimes switch to Italian, using the polite, distant form of "Lei," with a tone between shy and easygoing, which did not exclude a certain self-irony. He would give the same sarcastic look to anybody who condescendingly called him "Maestro," which was more precisely a form of address in the music world.

From the time he fled to the West, Nureyev's career was handled by the great impresario Sol Hurok. Then, for twenty-nine years by Sander Gorlinsky, the manager who had represented Callas. For the last ten years, Rudolf freed himself from contracts that were too binding. He preferred to entrust his career to a network of loving friends spread over Europe and the United States. They looked after his life, his performances, his houses, and his friendships. In France his all-time friends were Douce François and Mario Bois. They were fundamental to him, especially during the tempestuous period when he was directing the Ballet de l'Opéra de Paris. In England there were Maude Lloyd Gosling, an ex-ballerina and his biographer, and her husband, Nigel Gosling, who died in 1982. They wrote under the joint pseudonym of Alexander Bland. In the United States there were his friend Robert Tracy, and Andrew Grossman, the manager at United Artists who convinced him to debut in the musical *The King and I*. In Italy, Luigi Pignotti became his manager after having been his masseur and secretary for a long time. One day, when I was a member of the editorial staff of the magazine *Balletto Oggi*, Pignotti asked me to look after the foreign business and press relations in his Milan office. Anybody who, like me, belongs to the generation of children who were thunderstruck by dance, thanks to the most seductive of its princes, Nureyev can understand how attractive the offer was. I had seen the Nureyev of the great classics, in 1973, wide-eyed and from a box at La Scala, in an unforgettable *Giselle* with Carla Fracci. Obviously, I accepted. It was 1988.

"Work is my country. I was born with a suitcase in my hand." This was Nureyev's dictum. It reflected the ritual that was repeated each time. For example, there were four thousand spectators waiting to see him at the Coliseu in Lisbon, in July 1991.

As tour manager, I went with him, and lost 6.5 pounds in two days. He arrived from Vienna with the scores and his baton under his arm. He gave them to me at the airport. It was one of the countless shows that we promoted around the world under the name "Nureyev and Friends." The dancers who were to take part had arrived in Lisbon a few at a time. Among them were Evelyne Desutter, Andrej Fedotov and Umberto De Luca. At the last minute, Eric Vu An had decided not to come. When I told him, Rudolf was not pleased and commented with one of his most colorful epithets. The blond Andrej had lost his costumes in a suitcase somewhere, and we had to make do somehow. We found a blouse for *Don Quixote* in the repertory of a local company.

The dancers had to be loved and looked after like children. Their heads were often as high in the air as they leapt. Rehearsals began immediately at the Coliseu, which was a slightly run down arena. That little company made up of French, Russian, Italian, and Portuguese dancers had only a few hours to coalesce as a group and find a common identity to be able to appear in public as the Friends of Nureyev. On stage, Nureyev would correct the others while he walked the steps of the pieces that he would be dancing, Nijinski's *Après-midi d'un faune*, *The Lesson* by Flindt, and *The Moor's Pavane* by Limòn. As was the case in his later years, the mind was determined to execute all the variations in the most minute detail, often followed by a recalcitrant body. "Valeria, tell Evelyne that she also has to do the *pas de six* in *Flower Festival*." Desutter, *étoile* of reed-like grace, seemed to become even more ghostly while, bent over in the wings, she would massage her aching feet. "*Mais non, je ne peux pas*," she would murmur to me, her head bent, "I'm already on stage from beginning to end." Nureyev would go over to her with a half smile and not allow any objections. The stage-hands mounting the scenery for the *Faune* were impatient to go on break. I asked them not to break because there was very little time for rehearsals. Nureyev approached me. "Tell them to place the scenery higher. I want the public to see me when I am making love to myself." Only one thing worried him: "I don't want anyone stealing the costumes of *Faune* tonight. They belong to the production I danced with Margot." That night I slept with Fonteyn's nymphs locked in the cupboard of my hotel room. The following day Lisbon bowed before the old lion, Nureyev, and his Friends.

From time to time, the performances of the Friends were extemporaneous and rather homemade, and Nureyev's entire Italian management seemed like a family. All around, omnipresent and obliging, were the fans, women who had dedicated their lives to him with generosity and heedless hope. They were the lay nuns, immolated on the altar of their god. Women of every nationality and from every walk of life followed him around the world, some making great sacrifices to do so. They were often insistent, sometimes obsessive, for information about their idol. But they were satisfied with a glance, a word stolen outside the dressing room. When Nureyev died he left behind a trail of inconsolable widows.

During the reality of the work, the concrete rite of what it means to "manage" Nureyev alternated among ephemeral splendors and accounts that had to be balanced, encouraging dancers and organizing technical stage sets.

Dealing with him was like managing nitroglycerine. His fiery temperament was well-known. He had already given ample proof of it during his London period. Fonteyn herself confessed, "Rudolf has terrible mood swings. Sometimes he takes it out on others, but

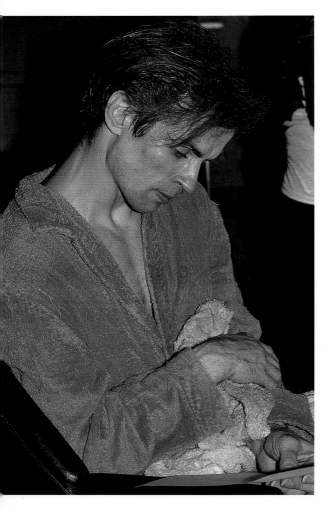

he doesn't mean it. His defects do not affect his professionalism." He would defend himself saying, "Unless one has a little temperament, a bit of passion, one is not alive." And during an interview in the seventies, Carla Fracci said, "He is very hard on himself. That must be respected. His style is strength and determination. His technical rigor has always helped me. Rudolf is a partner who is not limited to being a *porteur*, he is a dancer. He is right to be so temperamental. He requires everybody's collaboration and if he notices any signs of slacking, he makes everyone tremble. But he knows how to be very tender." At the Opéra de Paris, where he was director for eight years, the anecdotes were many. Elizabeth Platel remembers, "Everyone knows the story of the bottles of tea that he would throw into the air when we made a mistake. He would shout: 'This will not do!' and throw something in the air." Sylvie Guillem: "Nureyev did not need to dance. He would go into a bar and order a coffee and the earth would shake." Rudolf had a visceral, sanguine vision of work. "Every time you dance," he would say, "you must give your blood." But the muscles were only a means of expression. "I work and dance with my mental energy, and I dance better when I am tired." He was constantly at war with a body that was to be bent to his will. "When I work I can put myself to the test. I have to be faithful to what I do. Dance is my life." Apart from temperament, he could also be generous. He would show his younger colleagues the tricks of the trade, revealing secret techniques for the steps or the interpretative mysteries of a role.

This was the way he spent the four years, his last on the stage. He was strenuously determined to die there, where his home always had been—in the theatre. The illness that rendered him weak on the first night of his *Bayadère* in October 1992 was still carefully hidden. The people who were with him knew, but could never talk about it, because Nureyev did not want to talk about it. Every one of us, in our own way, tried to do as much as possible to create a barrier of protection around him, working for him and looking after him. Even that last flaming madness of conducting the orchestra, which he took on when his body could no longer withstand the rigors of the dance, seemed to him a dignified *buen retiro* for his unbounded talent.

After he had fled to the West, Nureyev was left, in fact, without a family. He was the eternal prodigal son. He was denied by his father Hamet, a political instructor in the Red Army. His mother did forgive him, but under duress. He managed, in a dramatic phone call ("Mother, ask me if I am happy"), to extort a benediction of his new life beyond the Iron Curtain. In Europe, Nureyev created a series of acquired families for himself, microcosms that affectionately revolved around him like the galaxies of a complex solar system. Among these elected families were Nigel and Maude Gosling in London, Charles Jude and Florence Clerc in Paris/Nice, and Luigi Pignotti in Milan.

Nureyev had an innate sense of humor which was sometimes insinuating and sometimes impertinent. He loved to create neologisms, scrambling the languages that he used the most: English, some regurgitation of Russian, of which he retained the epithets, most of which were incomprehensible, and French. He used them off the stage or during rehearsals in order to direct his army of dancers, who both feared and venerated him. He had a taste for the whiplash remark, which was the natural reflection of a cultured mind, and extraordinary in its intelligence. He shaped the words in his own image and likeness, mixing human, animal, and gastronomical allusions. He amused himself by dishing up puns that were often of a sexual nature.

He was provocative, like he was in the role of Basilio, the Gascon barber, in *Don Quixote*. He was exhilarating, and often pungent.

One evening he was stitching together the cast of his farewell tour in Australia, which was to perform in Melbourne, Newcastle, Brisbane, Sydney, and Adelaide. Nureyev arrived in Milan to meet the producer who, with his assistant, had just landed in a city that was strangely tropical for September. The Australians were still jet lagged. They treated Nureyev with deference, which was legitimate considering their lack of familiarity with this person whom they considered a *monstre sacré*. They proceeded to deal with the planning of the program. When it came to the choice of dancers, we suggested some of the best names from the Opéra de Paris and La Scala in Milan. And this was where the row began. For every name put forward Nureyev replied not with an appreciation of the dancer's work but with his sexual desirability in a possible amorous skirmish. The result was a desecrating, uncontrollable, impassioned outpouring worthy of an Indian erotic manual, with as many variations on the theme of male and female. When the two Australians had recovered from their first moment of disorientation, the embarrassment melted away and a collective laugh broke the stiff atmosphere of the evening. In spite of everything, and like a previously insoluble puzzle, the details of the tour were put together perfectly.

In his own way, and with the omnivorous ardor of an autodidact, Nureyev was an intellectual. He had refined taste. He appreciated tradition, the classics. He would throw himself voraciously into all the arts with the mind of a Renaissance man. At the same time, however, he was curious and wanted to experiment. His intellectual taste was not without the whiff of snobbism that came with the fact that he was often present when one precise and unrepeatable moment is celebrated. He had an accentuated sensibility toward cultural fashions. Rather than the fetishes of a superficial

vanity, he regarded them as precognitive signs of the enormous moving magma that is the social fabric of a particular era.

Nureyev was passionate about literature. He had a fatal attraction for Byron, the damned hero of Romanticism. He even played the part of Byron in *Manfred*, one of his rare, original choreographies. He studied Shakespeare with equal passion, so that he could mount his production of *Romeo and Juliet* with dramatic discipline. And he studied the sources that Shakespeare had used for this tragedy. Nureyev loved music and musicians. He knew Stravinsky personally and he directed Stravinsky's *Apollon Musagète* at Deauville. He adored the pianist Sviatoslav Richter, whom he had met in Russia at Khrushchev's dacia. He had a visceral passion for Glenn Gould, who was the first western musician to be invited to play in the Soviet Union. Nureyev was there to attend one of his concerts and was struck by how the pianist's emotive interpretation infused life into the music.

Nureyev's favorite instrument was the piano. And this meant the traveling Pianola that was bounced around with his caravanserai of suitcases in his adventurous tours around the world. A most noble harpsicord graced his apartment at Twenty-three Quai Voltaire in Paris. He had an antique organ brought by helicopter to the island of Li Galli. I remember that this event caused a certain amount of confusion in that miniature universe that is Positano. At the top of Nureyev's musical Olympus, however, was most definitely Bach. He jealously guarded the scores for the *Well-tempered Clavier* in one of the military sacks that he dragged around on his travels. So when the time came to chose the music for his funeral, it was natural that his friends, Mario Bois and André Larquié, decided on some passages from *The Art of Fugue*.

His love of art is manifest by the countless paintings, mostly eighteenth and nineteenth century, that covered the walls of his museum-like homes. He took advantage of his friendship with the set designer, Ezio Frigerio, to deepen his knowledge of the history of Italian art. He would overwhelm him with questions about the Renaissance, about painters, and architects that had left their mark.

He loved the cinema. On his rare evenings at home he would watch films by Chaplin, Eisenstein, or Lubitsch. His sensibility for the cinematographic image was powerfully present in his production in Hollywood of Cinderella, with its references to Fritz Lang's *Metropolis*, and to Chaplin. In the ballet he himself impersonated the producer, cigar hanging out of his mouth, a cross between Groucho Marx and Rothbart, the magician in *Swan Lake*. His imagination must have been fired during his time on the set of Ken Russell's *Valentino*.

In September 1991, he had flown from Li Galli to Milano and called ahead: "Valeria, please, La Scala and Urga." Decyphered,

this message meant concentration on two objectives with maximum urgency. The first was to continue negotiations with Carlo Fontana, superintendent at La Scala, for the choreographic rights to his classics: *Don Quixote, Swan Lake, The Nutcracker, Cinderella, Sleeping Beauty,* and *Romeo and Juliet.* The second objective was more personal but equally urgent. He wanted to see *Urga,* the film by Nikita Michalkov, which had been awarded the Golden Lion at the Venice Film Festival that had just concluded. The film was screened at the Colosseo cinema in viale Monte Nero in preview as part of a comprehensive exposition in Milan of the film festival. I went with Nureyev and Blue Robinson, the ex-sailing enthusiast who had just become his personal secretary. The manager of the cinema had been warned and, in a state of agitation, was there to meet us. The film was in its original Russian version with English subtitles, and this enabled Nureyev to fully immerse himself in the Russian steppe. There were landscapes of consuming melancholy, full shots of the barren countryside where nature is the savage master of man's destiny. The story is about the wanderings of two friends, a Mongol shepherd, Bayartu, and a Russian truck driver, Gostucin. I looked at Nureyev. He was huddled in his seat, legs sliding forward. The khaki hat was pulled down over his eyes. He seemed to be protected by the long raincoat that he was wearing. His gaze was lost, a thousand miles away, engrossed in the screen, traveling that barren land enveloped in an infinite sky. Magically, in that moment the severed umbilical cord with his country was healed. The connection had been violently broken by his escape at the Paris airport of Le Bourget long ago, in 1961. Now nostalgia began to flow once again. At the end of the film, still engrossed in the images of the film, he got up without a word, disturbed only by a RAI (RadioTelevisione Italiana) television film crew that had obviously been called by the manager of the cinema. We walked in silence toward the exit. I waited until we were in the taxi before speaking to him. Foolish move. Darkly, he said, "Don't talk to me." But after a few minutes he excused himself in his own way for that rude remark, and began joking about the taxi driver's driving.

Even in his greatest moments, Nureyev was haunted by the regret that his mother could not take part in his triumph. Nostalgia and solitude were the thrust towards the absolute, coupled, at a painful distance, with a secret sensitivity for the transcendental dimension. These were always recurrent themes in the life of Nureyev.

Strangely enough, the first poem that he ever learned at school, and which he remembered as an adult, was a lyric by the Russian, Michail Jurevic Lermontov, a poet in the style of Byron, who was killed in a duel. The poem is about a sailboat adrift on the deep blue sea. The poet does not know what the boat has lost, what it is looking for. It is simply immersed in its element. It goes for-

ward unhappily, restless. He brought with him from Russia a love for the poet Pushkin, and for Dostoyevski. He once said, "I would like to play the part of a Dostoyevski character. It would be wonderful to try and fail." He did try. He didn't fail. He succeeded: he danced *The Idiot*, a ballet by Panov, and found one of his greatest characters in Gogol's Akakij Akakjevič. He transformed the character into a concentrate of lyricism and heartrending melancholy, a Chaplinesque creature, a sublime loser. *The Overcoat*, choreographed by Flemming Flindt, was produced at the Pergola in Florence in 1989 with the Maggio Musicale Ballet Company. Nureyev had Austrian and French citizenship. He returned to Russia during the Gorbachev era, after Horowitz. After him, Rostropovic, another great artistic exile, was welcomed.

Until two years before his death, Nureyev was still embarrassingly beautiful. His attractiveness was something that stunned and amazed. In his youth, he had entire corps de ballets at his feet.

The actress Liz Robertson, his co-star in the musical *The King and I* in 1989, described this inescapable process of attraction very well. "Rudolf was so fascinating that being seen with him made you special. All he had to do was enter a room and the atmosphere would change. He was so beautiful that seeing him for the first time was almost a shock." He had an innate charisma on stage. It was as natural to him as breathing.

And yet, he would suddenly become very shy. I was once alone with him at lunch at Bagutta in Milan. I had gone to pick him up at the Grand Hotel Plaza in Largo Augusto. He would talk to me every day on the phone, but he was not used to seeing me. He was embarrassed and asked me, "Do you have lunch?" I replied, "Generally, yes," and he began to laugh. While we were at the restaurant I asked him for advice on the degree thesis I was preparing about him and his English period. I confessed to him, "They told me at the university that if I want to tackle the subject of ballet I would be on my own." He told me, "I help you. Go to London, talk to Ninette De Valois, founder of the Royal Ballet. Talk to the critic of *Time*, John Percival, and to Maude Gosling. And then go to Margot." And I did. I left for London with his *Petrushka* costume in my suitcase, and delivered it to Maude. I interviewed her and Percival. I met De Valois in her house in Richmond Park. She was deaf by this time, but still very lucid. To my great regret I did not manage to meet Margot Fonteyn. At the time, she was in Houston and would die not much later.

During that lunch at Bagutta, Nureyev ordered his favorite menu for his working days in Milan. Vegetable soup and rare filet steak, which he sent back to the chef three times until it was cooked as he wanted it. The game of the steak was something that often happened with him. Oriella Dorella, his partner in *The Lesson*, by

Flemming Flindt, remembered an evening with him. They were in a restaurant in Trieste. Asked by the desperate cook how he wanted his blessed steak cooked, he replied, "I want it with blue blood."

Every morning the routine was the same. Alarm at 9 to be ready at the theatre at 10. Then a class that lasted one and a quarter hours in Italy and one and a half hours in London, Paris, and Russia. The same rite would be repeated every day. Everybody, star and corps de ballet, at the barre, to stretch the muscles again, in strictest discipline.

Nureyev was a gypsy. He was always poised for departure. He was the most-traveled dancer in history. He would say, "Dance is my territory." But there was also an extra-territorial dimension. He was like James in *Sylphide*, who leaves his mortal destiny and his reassuring circle of friends to follow a seductive, but elusive spirit that forces him into an eternal pursuit and in the end disappears and leaves him alone. As far as love was concerned—the daily routine of it—it took second place in his existence. Even though he felt intense passions, like the devouring passion he had for Erik Bruhn, they enriched his interpretative qualities. Love, for him, was sublimated on stage in a miracle that was repeated every evening. "My whole being," he would say, "my entire existence is in the dance. But without love it is hard to exist."

Like in Béjart's *Chant du Compagnon Errant*, Nureyev was always forced to face an alter ago, an invisible and obstructive companion, to whom he had to report, and who pulled him this way and that. The Angel and the Devil co-habited in him.

Courage. A proud, straight and disarming look. That finger pointed, in *Giselle*, at Hilarion as he takes his sword, that could run him through with the greatest of ease. A concentration of virility and regal aggressiveness, from the pride that can kill but also can show mercy. These are metaphors for the recklessness and pugnacity of Nureyev. His face hollowed by illness, it was an act of supreme courage to appear before his public on the stage of the Opéra de Paris, on the first night of *La Bayadère*.

The troubled and self-destructive energy. Like Gustav Aschenbach, the professor of Thomas Mann's *Death in Venice*, Nureyev was pervaded by that sense of longing that pursues a form of absolute beauty, at the cost of showing his own personal decadence.

Nureyev was a man who kept his promises. I had asked him to give me an interview for my thesis. I followed him around all day, from a massage to a working lunch. I was only slightly encouraged to see that even the authoritative critic of "Le Figaro" René Sirvin, had been given the same cavalier treatment. There was, for Nureyev, a sort of democratic equality among those who surrounded him.

There were no first places. The Danish choreographer, Flemming Flindt, had freely adapted the ballet from *Death in Venice*. That muggy evening, 25 May 1991, at the Teatro Filarmonico in Verona, Nureyev was Gustav Ashenbach, the writer who is hopelessly in love with the adolescent Tadzio. In the interval between the first and second acts, Nureyev called me to his dressing room. Knowing how impatient he was with the curiosity of the press, it must have been torture for him, but with great patience and discipline, he submitted to my interview. There were many questions, particularly regarding his English period. When the stage manager knocked on the door, calling out, "On Stage!," an order that performers have to obey, Nureyev was unperturbed. He continued to answer my questions, seated at the mirror retouching his makeup. Five minutes later the scene was repeated. The stage manager called him a second time, and then a third time. Laughing, he was still unmoved. "Maestro, the public are all seated, they are waiting for you . . .". That evening he said to me, "I have been a natural performer. I don't know which was for the better and which was for the worse. Or maybe it has all been for the better, performing in many pieces and in many different roles. Variety springs from comedy to drama. I was born for this. To be a chameleon."

From this freeze-frame, this harbinger of the most painful moments of Nureyev's life, the lens now turns back, along the tracks of the Trans-Siberian train, to a day long ago, 17 March 1938.

A Legend Born on a Train for Vladivostok

A rushing train makes its way, puffing across a landscape rendered barren by the ice, in an unnamed territory in northern Mongolia. The train races across the steppe. The mechanical locomotion of the train does not make the nature of the place less unreal. Here, at the ideal point between two coordinates traced by destiny, Lake Baikal on one side and the city of Irkutsk on the other, Rudolf Hametovic Nureyev was born on 17 March, 1938.

His mother was to join her husband, Hamet, a political instructor of the Red Army, at the garrison in Vladivostok, the most extreme point of the Russian continent that stretches from Manchuria toward the Sea of Japan. There, where the West melts into the East, Nureyev was born. He was traveling, as destiny would have it, even before he was born, on the Trans-Siberian railway, the route of mass wanderings, a land that was itself a new frontier.

Nureyev was born at the height of the Stalin purges, when millions of people were sent to gulags in Siberia. Stalin ordered spectacular trials and campaigns against the opposition. The year following Nureyev's birth, 1939, the pact between Hitler and Stalin decreed that the Baltic states, eastern Poland, and Bessarabia should

pass under the control of Russia. And in 1941 Germany attacked the Soviet Union and suffered her first defeat at the battle for Moscow. It was in this period that Rudolf was taking his first steps, in a country lacerated by poverty and war.

His family belonged to the Baskskir ethnic group, an Asian branch with Muslim roots. They were descendants of ancient warriors that invaded Russia between the thirteenth and fourteenth centuries. The family name was originally Fasli, then in his grandfather's time it became Nuri, owing to an error of transcription at the registry of births and deaths. His father, Hamet, was a simple non-commissioned officer in the Russian Army. His mother, Farida Agilivuljevna Nureyevna, of Kazak origin, had begun her voyage to join her husband, with her three daughters, Rosa, Lylia, and Razida.

The journey to Vladivostok was interminable. At the time, it took ten days to get there from Moscow. The birth of a son would have crowned Hamet's desire to have a future companion for hunting and fishing. When the third daughter was born, Farida was afraid to tell him that it was a girl. Now, to the great pride of the Red Army instructor who never wanted to pose for photographs without his medals, a son had arrived. The announcement came via the telegraph office in Irkutsk. The family returned to Moscow before war broke out, and in 1941 Hamet was sent to the front. Farida, Rosa, Lylia, Razida, and the little Rudolf were forced to evacuate under the bombardments, and they fled to Chicuna, a small village near the city of Ufa.

These were years of hunger and the fear of wolves. In 1943 they moved to Ufa, guests of an uncle, into a tiny one-room house of 129 square feet. The bathroom was under the stars. What little there was, was divided with another family. Mother and children managed as best they could, washing bottles, collecting copper coins, selling old newspapers. It was a great feast when their father sent cocoa from the front. Their mother was a hardworking and courageous woman. Once, she was even attacked by wolves as she was returning home, and she managed to chase them away by setting fire to a blanket.

During this childhood of unhappiness and misery, something happened before Rudolf's eyes, and the image would never leave him. It was 1 January 1945. His mother took her seven-year-old son to the local theatre to see a performance of *The Song of the Cranes*, which was a ballet inspired by an exotic fable with a patriotic background.

Rudolf realized that this was his world and that dance would be his destiny. He was encouraged by his mother and his sister Rosa, the intellectual of the family, who was later to go to the college. He began to attend groups of country dancing. His father returned home when Rudolf was eight, and dreamed of him becoming a doctor, or an engineer, with a technical education, with his "feet on the ground." The irony was that the soldier who venerated Stalin should be confronted by an urchin who jumped and danced at home all the time, and was unwilling to take part in any of the pastimes that Hamet loved, like hunting. In the meantime, Rudolf began to appear in amateur folklore productions.

It was then that Anna Udeltsova offered him help. She had been part of Diaghilev's Ballets Russes, and had become the central point in Ufa for amateur ballet. She was to be the first in a long line of generous women who were to help Nureyev in his career. Under the sure guide of Udeltsova, Rudolf made remarkable progress and after just one year he was able to take lessons with an ex-dancer from the Kirov, a friend of Anna's. He was forced to take lessons in secret. His father disapproved and did not see why Rudolf wanted to be a professional dancer. It was even considered eccentric in Russia for a man to be a dancer.

Later he would remember. "Everybody told me that I had talent, but I soon realized that no one would actually take me by the hand and guide me. I was alone and had to decide everything for myself. And that is what I have always done." His ideas were clear. He auditioned in Moscow for the great maestro Asaf Messerer, who then made him the attractive offer of admission to the eighth grade at the Bolshoi school. This was the course that he would have had to attend if he had begun his studies eight years earlier at that school. Nureyev refused because the school did not have living facilities for the students, who had to find and pay for their own accommodations. When he returned to Ufa he had made his decision. There was only one academy for him. This was the Vaganova Choreography Institute, which was attached to the Kirov in Leningrad and called the Marinskji of St. Petersburg, as it was named in the Tsarist era. Leningrad was re-baptised St. Petersburg after perestroika. This was the theatre from which the brightest stars of Russian ballet came: Vaslav Nijinski, Anna Pavolva, Tamara Karsavina, George Balanchine. All over the world the Kirov was and still is a name that evokes a crystalline purity of technique and refined interpretation. The Vaganova Academy also offered Rudolf an additional concrete economic advantage. It guaranteed him a place to live.

Nureyev collected three thousand rubles by teaching dance at the local fairs and managed to buy a one-way ticket to Leningrad. It was a morning in August 1955.

From Folk to Classic Dance: Objective Kirov

The banks of the Neva. A barre attached to a mirror—making a connection between Ufa and Leningrad. Nureyev was there to face his first challenge. Not by chance, this was to coincide with his first explosive collision with authority. From the beginning it was mortification. The seventeen-year-old savage from the provinces was put into the sixth grade, which was taught by the head of the school, Valentin Chelkov. The course was for fifteen year olds. The prelude, admission day, 24 August 1955, was not encouraging. He was told by the examiner, Vera Kostravitskaja, "Dear young man, you can either become a great dancer or be a total failure. Personally I would opt for the second hypothesis." The challenge had begun. An almost military discipline reigned in the academy and Nureyev was forced to bow to the regulations. But not completely. In order to become a real dancer he thought he should attend the Kirov performances. He secretly managed to see *Taras Bul'ba*. He was punished for this insubordination when he returned to the boarding school. After a fiery encounter with the severe Chelkov, he asked the head of the school, Nicolai Ivanovski, to admit him to Aleksandre Pushkin's lessons (the same name as the poet), in the eighth grade. Pushkin was a good man, open and sensitive. He accepted Nureyev gladly, and took him under his wing. As a young man Pushkin had been a great dancer, but of little presence, and his dancing classes were the best in the entire school. Thanks to his teaching, Nureyev improved daily. He said later, "He taught me the art of enriching every sequence with emotion." The attentive eye of Pushkin had seen in Nureyev an actor who could embody the nuances of an interpretation. At the end of the course, Nureyev had an opportunity to show off the results of his studies with a test that he had prepared. He chose a concentration of virtuosity and acrobatics in the variation of the *pas de deux* from *Diana and Atteone*, choreographed by Vachtang Chabukiani, and taken from the ballet *Esmeralda*.

In Leningrad he used his free time to improve his education. He would spend whole days at the Hermitage and at the Russian Museum. He cultivated his passion for the paintings of Van Gogh, the works of Dostoevesky, and the music of Scriabin.

He had a friendship with a Cuban companion at school, Menia Martinez, with whom he would scan copies of *Dance Magazine*. A friend of hers used to send them from London. From those pages, he could study the stars of dance in the West: Margot Fonteyn and Erik Bruhn, in particular.

In 1958 he graduated from the Kirov school and won the Moscow pan-Soviet competition, with a variation, *Corsair*, that was to become his war-horse in the West. His entrance was like a bomb ready to explode. The applause made the theatre ring. He was offered admission to the corps de ballet of three companies: the Stanislavski theatre, which Nureyev considered to be too provincial; the Bolshoi which could offer him partnership with prima ballerinas of the caliber of Galina Ulanova and Maja Plissetskaya; and the Kirov.

Nureyev made his debut at the Kirov on 25 October 1958. He danced the pas de trois from *Swan Lake* with Nina Jastrebova and Galina Ivanova. Then his career began to take off. The Ukrainian dancer, Natalia Dudinskaja, was the forty-six-year-old prima ballerina of the Kirov. She had gracefully survived the generation of Konstantin Sergeev and Vachtang Chabukiani. She chose Nureyev as the lead in the ballet *Laurencia* by Krejn-Chabukiani. Dudinskaja was the wife of Sergeev, the director of the Kirov from 1951, and she was very powerful. For Nureyev the role was like a promotion.

In 1959, an hour or so before the curtain rose on the second performance of *Laurencia*, an accident nearly interrupted his promising career. He broke the ligaments of his right knee during a rehearsal. He was so frightened by the thought of resting for two years, as he had been diagnosed, that he was back after a month, thanks to the care and attention he received from Pushkin, in his own home.

He was back on the boards. As lead dancer. He had a taste for risk. He eliminated the mimed parts. He even left the stage in the middle of a scene because he did not have to dance at that moment. "I am a dancer, not a mime" was his answer, not his justification. The public began to enjoy the risk that he brought to his interpretations and he created a lot of excitement. On the other hand, the purists were furious. He lifted his legs like only the ballerinas did. The effect, however, was not feminine, but "exotic."

Biographer Gennadyj Smakov remembers, "He was the first to make a three quarters grand pirouette on point to make his legs look longer. It was a trick that infuriated the purists, but when Baryshnikov did it fifteen years later it seemed to be part of the routine." These were not the only innovations that Nureyev introduced to the Kirov. The use of costumes changed radically. Nureyev insisted on transparent tights, which was scandalous for the time. He refused the puffed pantaloons that made the line look heavy. For this reason a production of *Don Quixote* became a bone of contention. Something similar had happened some dozen years before to Nijinski. He, too, was accused, and caused a scandal when he pointed out that costumes catalyzed the attention of the public.

Nureyev's rise within the company was rapid, but he was dancing too little, only three or four times a month. What followed was a series of disagreements with the theatre. They accused him of spending too much time with foreigners and of an excessive interest in non-Soviet shows. The situation did not improve when the Kirov sent him and a group of soloists to Vienna to the youth festival. The French choreographer Roland Petit saw him for the first time in Vienna and described him as a young Cossack ready to explode. On his return, Nureyev missed the train for Moscow.

Discipline had been broken. Things did not improve during a succession of tours in Berlin, where he bought a piano that was then confiscated by the KGB when he was condemned *in absentia* for treason.

In the summer of 1960 he was asked by Ninel Kurgapkina to dance the adagio of the *pas de deux* from *Don Quixote* at the dacia of Nikolai Alekandrivoch Bulganin. It was an entertainment in honor of Khrushchev, and the pianist Svjatoslav Richter and the composer Dimitri Shostakovic were also present. This was an encounter with power that was the prelude to a direct confrontation.

Escape to the West: the Rebel Becomes a Star

Six steps toward freedom, taken with a measured but iron determination. On 17 June, 1961 Nureyev burst into the homes of half the world through their television sets. The fearless Russian was a fugitive. The rebellious dancer, who was just twenty-three years of age, had turned his back on Khrushchev and opted to stay in Paris.

The performances in Vienna, Egypt, and Berlin had been his first real experiences of a non-Soviet public. At the time, not only Berlin but the whole world was divided into two opposing blocs by the Cold War.

Emblematically, 1961 was the same year that Russian cosmonaut Yuri Gagarin became the first man in space. When Nureyev debuted in *La Bayadère*, the Parisian public re-named him "Sputnik" because of his ability to fly. Thirty one years later, on the stage of the Palais Garnier, his final farewell to Paris was to be with the same ballet.

Today, Le Bourget airport in Paris is reserved for private flights. But it made history on that sunny day in June 1961, when an artistic and political exception was made that reverberated in every corner of the world. At that time Le Bourget was the largest airport in Paris. Nureyev has told the story hundreds of times. After all, he said, he was born that day. When he arrived at the airport, a representative of the Kirov told him that there was no seat for him on the flight to London. Amazement, perplexity, disappointment, and, in the end, suspicion. Why would they leave him behind after he had recently been a hero in Paris? A last minute substitution? No, they explained, reassuring him, his destination was to be Moscow where there was an important occasion waiting for him. Khrushchev wanted to see him dance at the Kremlin. But there was no program, no costumes. They would arrange something when they got there. It was clear that they wanted to get rid of him. He was too undisciplined, a rebel, and always so fatally attracted to foreigners. The time had come for Rudolf to be afraid and to say good-bye to his dreams of freedom. There was no way out. He

turned to some French friends. They immediately formed a network of cooperation and set about finding out how he could request political asylum. It was simple. He was to take six slow steps, and pronounce the fateful phrase, "I would like to stay in your country." And that was the way it happened. No breathless race, no sensational leap. Only six steps. Hidden behind a pillar, Nureyev managed to elude both the representatives of the company and the agents of the KGB who had been following him during that stay in Paris. He was able to reach the French officials. When he declared his request for asylum, he was sent to the airport offices, where he was to spend forty-five minutes. It seemed like an eternity. When the Soviets realized what he had done, they were stunned. It was the first case of a Russian dancer fleeing to the West. They knocked on the door, they shouted threats at him, promises, reassurances. Nureyev signed the French document assisted by an interpreter who tried to dissuade him. It certainly was a risk. He would be alone, without any money, not even a suitcase. The press immediately began to focus on Nureyev. They asked him if his decision had been political, artistic, or maybe, sentimental. His ties with Russia and with his family had been severed definitively. He would be considered a traitor and they would cancel him from national memory, dishonored.

For years, not even his family knew exactly what had happened in Paris. Nureyev had been swallowed up beyond the Curtain and, for his relations, he no longer existed. Those in Russia who had always supported and helped him reacted either by understanding the reasons or by repudiating him. For his father it was a terrible dishonor.

This was a time of great confusion for Nureyev. He was threatened by the KGB on the one hand; besieged by entreaties to return on the other. From an FBI report published in 1999 it was discovered that the Americans also thought he was a potential Russian spy. That state of uncertainty, however, was resolved within a few days. The Ballet of the Marquis de Cuevas, a prestigious traveling company, offered him a contract for six years. Nureyev thought the period was too long, and signed for three months. Some days after his break with the Kirov, he was dancing in *Sleeping Beauty* in Paris.

His thoughts, however, were elsewhere. They were in Denmark, where Erik Bruhn was working. To Nureyev, Bruhn was the best dancer in the world. His thoughts were also in the United States, where a great Russian, George Balanchine, had formed the New York City Ballet into a model of perfection. In Copenhagen he tried to learn from Bruhn all the secrets of the *danseur noble*. He rehearsed with him and went to his performances. The respect between them transformed into a friendship, and then a love affair.

But another city was looming on the horizon. This was London, where the first lady of English ballet, Margot Fonteyn, invited him to join the Royal Ballet.

The break with Moscow was healed twenty-six years later, when, in the renewed climate of perestroika, Gorbachev opened a path for him. His mother, Farida, was seriously ill. In 1987, Nureyev was given permission to go back to Russia to see her. On his arrival in Moscow he was met by a crowd of journalists. The television showed him in a state of grace. At last he could set foot in the museum of the Kirov where, mysteriously, among the photographs of Karsavina and Nijinsky, some of Nureyev seemed to have appeared. They had been hidden for years. There were emotional meetings and embraces. His teacher Anna Udeltsova, now a hundred years old, forgave him. His mother was being looked after by her daughters and hardly recognized him.

After that private visit, there came, for Nureyev, a great emotional moment—his re-entry on the stage of the Kirov. In November 1989 Oleg Vinogradov, director of the Kirov, invited him to join his old company to dance *Sylphide* in St. Petersburg.

This was a dream that Nureyev had hardly ever dared to imagine. He had been an Austrian citizen since 1982. He was fifty-one years old. His partner was the young Zanna Ajupova, who remembered that day. "When the curtain went up I began to dance, but I couldn't hear the music for the noise of the applause." Even if the great Nureyev had lost the shine of his best days, it was a triumph appreciated by twenty-five minutes of applause.

London, Vienna, Milan: Lift to Glory

Deferential and impassioned, Rudolf Nureyev kneels at the feet of Margot Fonteyn. He kisses her hand in front of the curtain at Covent Garden. The public goes crazy; the photographers go mad. Thus was born the legend of Nureyev/Fonteyn, the couple that pierced London's heart.

It was a risk that became the greatest winning bet of all the partnerships of the twentieth century. He was twenty-four; she was forty-three.

Fonteyn had begun her career with Robert Helpmann, who was her principal partner until the mid-fifties. Then she danced with Michael Soames, a good-looking dancer, strong and sure and well considered. A little while before the arrival of Nureyev, Soames had decided to retire from most of his roles and leave the classical repertory. In the interim, Fonteyn danced sporadically with other partners, among whom, principally, was David Blair. But they did not seem to be well matched, and the partnership did not work. The arrival of Nureyev was, therefore, greeted with relief because Fonteyn had at last found a partner who fitted her like a glove. Everybody agreed that their national star had never danced better. The effect of Nureyev on her and on the entire company was visible and even audible.

The change was profound on both sides. Nureyev modeled himself on the style of the English company that had accepted him, although he wanted to impose his own will and his own choices.

An exchange between Nureyev and Natalia Makarova is emblematic. She was also a refugee from Russia when they danced together for the first time in the West, in a pas de deux for television. During rehearsals Makarova, who had danced with him in the days of the Kirov, said to him, "You dance like them!" Rudolf replied, "No, I dance like myself." The influence of western choreographers on his style was obvious. The Russian school and the British school had fused together. On a silver platter, the West offered him the possibility to widen his expressive horizons, without losing anything that he had made treasure of from the Kirov. "I dance what I think, how I think and how I feel," he said in a strong Russian accent just after his flight in 1961.

Nureyev's impact on the Royal Ballet was stunning; some people thought it was destructive. The Russian became a model for the other dancers. He challenged them to raise their standards and ended by making the company stronger.

For Ninette De Valois, Nureyev was the reason to test the basis on which she had founded her company. Special prices were adopted for the appearance of the Nureyev/Fonteyn pairing. At first the press was electrified. Then the criticism and fault-finding began. Some journalists attacked Nureyev's performances. He tried to leap higher than anyone else, and the stage at Covent Garden was old and noisy. In some roles he seemed to land with a crash. Other critics objected that the modifications to the ballets would distort the repertory of the Royal Ballet. Nureyev's behavior away from the theatre did nothing to quell the clamor of the press. The gossips were always hungry for scandals, real or false, and added fuel to the news items. For a long time Nureyev did not have an easy time with the English press, nor with the American media. The "old guard" of Anglo-Saxon critics interpreted the innovative energy of Nureyev-Fonteyn as the collapse of what was considered as the British establishment. They underlined the marked contrast in their ages. The opinion of John Martin was also harsh. He was the seventy-year-old doyen of the *New York Times*. After the New York debut of Nureyev with Fonteyn and the Royal Ballet, he wrote that the prince in *Swan Lake* could easily be the most boring character conceived by a choreographer, but that Nureyev, who could not resist leaving the part unaltered, had managed to make him really offensive. Martin also expressed his regret and embarrassment at seeing the young Russian partnered with Fonteyn,

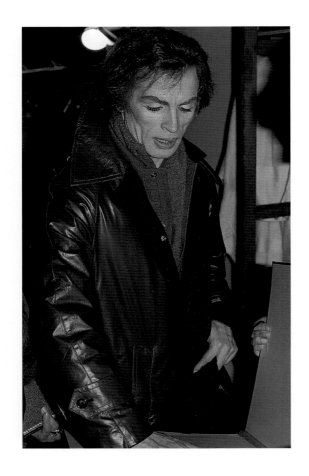

and added that it seemed like watching the first lady of English ballet going to the grand ball with a gigolo. The reply was not long in coming. Arnold Haskell, an equally authoritative ballet critic, gave battle in the pages of *Dancing Times*, writing dryly that Martin's article confirmed what he had long suspected, which was that his colleague understood nothing about ballet.

It was obvious that the arrival of the turbulent young man upset not only certain aesthetic canons of the most demanding critics, but certain very nationalistic sentiments. In fact, beyond the argumentative tone of the critics, there was a feeling of perplexity and concern for Fonteyn, who was unanimously considered the royal representative of English ballet, and the epitome of the British aristocratic class in the artistic field. She represented the most exquisite incarnation of that feeling of English understatement. All this was diluted by the showers of praise and favorable articles by other critics. Opposites co-habitated and Nureyev was an artist who lived extremes.

Expectations of the dancer who came from the East were very high. Evening after evening the public realized that what they saw on the stage was a rocket ready to launch into another pyrotechnical game. The dichotomy of the English press continued, one way or another, throughout Nureyev's career. The critics that had been hostile to his appearing on the English stage, ended up, in his last years, attacking him again for his devoted fidelity to dance. During both periods, the dawn and the sunset of his career, the English press behaved in a very contradictory manner. It was unbridled adulation or pitiless criticism.

Nureyev taught his English colleagues how to instill more strength, and dynamism into their performances. From them he learned the artfulness of acting. There were considerable differences between the two schools. Nureyev said later, with pride and a touch of snobbism, "Russians are natural dancers; the English have to learn." Dance and recitation fused in him. No comparison with other stars, like Nijinsky, could be made.

The art of the curtain call was perfected right from the first appearance of Nureyev-Fonteyn. Together at the proscenium, she holds a bouquet of roses, he, the stage ham, "feels" the warmth of the public, kneels at her feet, and kisses her hand with infinite gratitude. The effect on the public was so electrifying that they decided to rehearse their exits, which became more romantically ceremonious. Thus the applause became a show within a show.

In 1964 the relationship with the Royal Ballet faltered. Sudden engagements rained down and concentration declined. At first Rudolf felt he was lost, like he was during his first days in Paris after his request for political asylum. It was for him, however, an extraordinary moment to escape from London and seek new opportunities. So he began to mount his *Swan Lake* at the Staatsoper in Vienna. There followed *Don Quixote*, then *Sleeping Beauty* at Teatro alla Scala of Milan, *Nutcracker* in Stockholm, and then *Don Quixote* again in Zurich. There could be a career outside Covent Garden, and his horizons expanded.

At La Scala in Milan he found a new home, and a new partner in Carla Fracci. He said, "I don't know if home is in London or Paris or Milan or Vienna. I live out of my suitcase." On 9 October 1965 he debuted with Margot Fonteyn and the Royal Ballet at La Scala. The Nobel Laureate Eugenio Montale wrote of Nureyev in the *Corriere d'Informazione*: "Agile as an imp, vertiginous like a spinning top, apparently almost infantile, with an elegance that is never affected, he is a Romeo who has no other imaginable equal." Nureyev had already danced with Carla Fracci a couple of years earlier at the Teatro dell'Opera in Rome in a program in which the *étoile* from Milan was partnered first by Erik Bruhn in a *pas de deux* from *Romeo and Juliet*, and then by the Russian in *Sylphide*. After the performance, there was to be an exclusive society ball at Palazzo Colonna organized by Ira Fürstenberg for the Roman nobility. Carla Fracci, who has always considered herself the heir to Margot Fonteyn, continued the long road laid out by her illustrious English colleague. Fracci-Nureyev danced all over the world. Between the Metropolitan and La Scala, they performed about 160 ballets, from *Giselle* to *Swan Lake*, *Nutcracker*, *Don Quixote*, *Sylphide*, and *Sleeping Beauty*, all over the world, and then *Romeo and Juliet*, of which there is a version in video, with Margot Fonteyn in the role of Madonna Capuleti, choreographed by Nureyev himself.

At La Scala the Nureyev effect was as explosive as it had been in London. His name electrified the box office. Reservations were being accepted sixty days before opening night. In the case of his *Sleeping Beauty* with Carla Fracci, the empty seats in the stalls and boxes were gone in a day or two. The Nureyev effect had also hit Italy.

The Years of Transgression and the Jet Set

A helmet of straight hair, cut geometrically. When Nureyev landed in London he immediately absorbed the dictates of Anglo-Saxon fashion. In 1964 the *coiffeur* Vidal Sassoon had launched a new way of hair styling. With respect to the fifties, it was revolutionary. After the back combing and brilliantine, hair returned to its natural self, modern and even futuristic. Fashionable London submitted to Sassoon's five-point cut, a smooth, short helmet, with a fringe that cut the head horizontally above the ears. Mary Quant, the inventor of the miniskirt, was among the first important people to adopt it. The Beatles wore the longer version, the "mush-

room." At the time, it was considered scandalous that they should wear this style in their 1964 film *A Hard Day's Night*.

A mythical hairstyle reflected the desire to leave his mark on history through fashion. Nureyev began to appear with the same hairstyle as early as 1963. A New York newspaper described him as "a tiger who needed a good haircut." A standard bearer, therefore, or a fashion victim ahead of his time? Or was he, as a urban legend would have it, the inventor of the helmet hairstyle, which was then stolen by the Beatles? Fashion has always been a chain of connections between the trends in the street and the formal genre of the stylists.

During Nureyev's English years, London was living in the ferment of the first youth movements. In the spring of 1964 there was the clash between the mods, young people from the popular areas, and the rockers, who represented a more conservative and nostalgic position.

Those were the years when some myths were consumed in concentrated doses. John F. Kennedy became president in 1960 and was assassinated only three years later. In 1960, Hitchcock's *Psycho* was released, and the Guggenheim Museum of New York was inaugurated. In 1961, when Nureyev made his leap, the government of the German Democratic Republic began construction on the Berlin wall. And, curiously, the railroad on which he was born, the Trans-Siberian, was made electric. The fast pace of those years also influenced sexual behavior, with the arrival on the market of the revolutionary contraceptive pill in 1961. In 1962, the myth of James Bond was being born with the first film, *Dr. No*, directed by Terence Young and starring Sean Connery. And that year Marilyn Monroe's star faded with her suicide. While in 1964 the winds of war beat on Vietnam, pop art was exploding, and blacks saw Martin Luther King, Jr. being awarded the Nobel Prize. The Beatles were everywhere, and across the Atlantic, in 1965, Bob Dylan and Joan Baez were becoming the singers of the pacifist movement.

In the fabulous sixties, the decade of the Beatles and the Kennedys, there was a "Nureyev style," aggressive, nonconformist, eccentric. On stage the Russian was a demigod; on the streets he was followed and idolized. In a word, for better or for worse, he had the status of a pop star.

The phenomenon was of such proportions that the British press defined ballet fans as "Nureyevniks", an analogy to the Beatniks, or admirers of the Beat Generation. A court of adoring friends from the jet set now began to form around Rudolf. The circle of lovers, of both sexes, widened. He would say, "Knowing what it means to make love like a man and like a woman is a fundamental experience that should be communicated on stage."

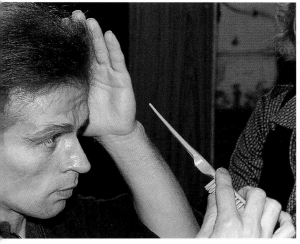

He confirmed the allure of eccentricity even before royalty. In a photograph taken at the Royal Academy in London in 1968, he is seen escorting Princess Margaret. He shows off thigh-high suede boots, a Russian-style jacket, and long hair. At the Acropolis in Athens he appeared before King Constantine and Queen Anne-Marie of Greece, and Princess Irene and Prince Michael, wearing a blue and white, horizontally striped suit and matching hat. With regard to hats, at a dinner hosted by Grace Kelly, he was asked to leave his hat at the coatroom. "I go with it!" he threatened. The ex-ragamuffin was now invited by President Carter and admitted to the White House. He was introduced into the exclusive circle of friends of the most powerful families in America such as the Kennedys and the Rothschilds. The Greek ship owner, Niarchos, invited him on his cruises.

In the era of the jet set, subsequent to that of the Roman *dolce vita*, Nureyev was one of the victims of the Italian *paparazzi*, constantly being photographed in night clubs.

He appreciated the natural ease of the American style. He said, "Dance is a process of the liberation of the body; we must stop being so controlled and enjoy the pleasure of movement. I think that the Americans, more than anyone else, are in a position to understand this by the way they move with such ease. It's the old story that dance has a liberating function. Everything begins with rock." And he was photographed in the sixties dressed like a rock star. Various hair styles, but above all berets, cloches, and fur hats. Nureyev's favorite wardrobe accessories were his boots—with vertiginous wedges, slavishly faithful to the fashion of the time. There were dozens of Nehru-style jackets and python suits, shoes included. On American television as a guest of Dick Cavett, he appeared in boots and jacket of python and a hairstyle à la an English knight. The fire red, plasticized duster coats, the military jackets, the furs of mink and seal, the braiding, all contributed to accentuate his Tartar fascination, in a celebrated photograph taken by Zoe Dominic he is a fascinating show-off, wearing a fur hat, while Julie Andrews playfully hides herself in his mink-lined trench coat. Again dressed in fur, he modeled for Blackgama with Martha Graham and Margot Fonteyn. The slogan of the advertising campaign was "What Becomes a Legend Most?" a question that would be hard to answer today. He was always at home with stylists. In Paris he would visit Yves Saint Laurent; in Milan Versace and Missoni.

On the Riviera in 1973 he was photographed on the beach, showing off his body in breathtakingly tight-fitting briefs with suspenders. Some months later, at a cocktail party for the Dance Magazine Awards, with Erik Bruhn, the greatest love of his life, he flaunted a Mick Jagger hairstyle and a black, double-breasted suit with a hussar collar. In 1977, in Paris at Maxim's, he was immor-

talized by *Paris Match* while clasped in a tango with Natalia Makarova. She was wearing a long white dress with dizzyingly high-heeled sandals; he was wearing one of his famous military-style suits. Once again on the dance floor, he was captured in the company of Elizabeth Taylor going wild in a twist. She was wearing a bell-shaped dress decorated with a feather. He had on a very tight black jacket and a white crew-necked sweater.

At the New York premiere of his film *Don Quixote*, shot with the Australian Ballet, he was dressed in suede from head to foot, a leather trench coat under his arm. The tops of his high boots were folded down in the "heroic Spaniard" effect. The buttons were visible on his pants, and he wore an ample belt.

In San Francisco the *paparazzi* surprised him sitting on a bench in the police station, looking threatening. He and Margot Fonteyn had been arrested at a party during a drug raid.

At the end of the sixties, Nureyev's off-stage look resembled the slave, as in Boris Godunov: mink down to his feet and crimson Scottish shawls. Underneath he wore white: a white high-necked sweater and white socks inside the high, very white boots. The photographers for whom he posed were Lord Snowdon, ex-husband of Princess Margaret, Cecil Beaton, Henri Cartier-Bresson, Elliot Erwitt, Serge Lido, Jacques Moatti, Colette Masson, Irving Penn, and Richard Avedon.

Nureyev loved nightlife, but he did not only go to important parties. He would also go to clubs and meeting places for men, such as the Club Baths in New York. Nureyev's homosexuality was obvious, but never put on show. He often inspired the gay imagination, becoming an icon in the gallery of world stars. In his video clip *I Want to Break Free*, Freddie Mercury could only have been thinking of Nureyev as he copied a faun-like Nijinski, and sang surrounded by a group of assorted nymphs. Years later, in a scandal mongering biography it was insinuated that there had been a relationship between Nureyev and Freddie Mercury. In 1974, the gay New York magazine *Dilettante*, dedicated to the arts, entertainment, and male sexuality, chose him for the cover of its first issue. The article inside was edited by the managing director, John Devere. It was called *In the spotlight: Nureyev*. It described him as a provocative paradox. The long article carried the allusive title "Nureyev and the Double-Edged Muse", while the pages that followed contained articles about New York strip artists, male cabarets and a guide to gay nightclubs "Night Life for the Pansexual."

At the end of the seventies, Nureyev began a relationship with Robert Tracy, a dancer who was then twenty-three. It began in New York during rehearsals for *Le Bourgeois gentilhomme* by Balanchine. On 30 January 2003 in the *Guardian* Tracy remembered the three years he spent with Nureyev as a mix of "dance, sex, and caviar."

Even in later years the icon Nureyev was much courted. In 1989 he appeared on the stamps of the Philatelic Agency of San Marino, when they dedicated to him the second series of "Great Personages." The first series portrayed Federico Fellini and Laurence Olivier.

A Talent in Cinema, Art and the Musical

Turban, hookah, and the blonde Michelle Phillips in his arms, was the way Nureyev became Valentino in the film directed by Ken Russell in 1977. The story of Nureyev and the cinema is full of long chases, temporary ambushes, sporadic bag snatching, and interminable waiting. The movies courted him. He became, for a while, one of their constant images. His facial expressions were as mobile as a river during a flood, changing all the time. His moods were variable and versatile.

He is the icon hanging on the wall of a Parisian room in François Truffaut's 1970 film, *Domicile Conjugale*. Claude Lelouch stole his most media-grabbing act, that of his "leap" to the West, whereas it was, in fact, a measured walk into the arms of the French police. In his film, *Les uns et les autres* (Bolero) in 1980, he has the Argentine Jorge Donn, dancer-symbol of Maurice Béjart, execute a *grand jeté* in the great square of the Esplanade.

As Nureyev recalled in 1966, Franco Zeffirelli wanted him to play the lead in a film on the life of a dancer. "I will make a film with Zeffirelli next summer, between June and August. It will be the story of a dancer today. He will be one of us, with the same problems that every dancer has in his career." The project did not materialize and the film was never made. A series of meetings took place. The Florentine director had taken on the legacy of Visconti, who had been very friendly with Carla Fracci. Sometimes the encounters between Zeffirelli and Nureyev were fiery. One ended in a furious quarrel that, some time later, was patched up with a friendly exchange of ideas. The incident was put aside with a good laugh, as often happened after a show of temperament by Nureyev. As chance would have it, the Russian, who had become the owner of Li Galli, also became Zeffirelli's neighbor.

In 1972 in Melbourne, Nureyev debuted as a film director with the Australian Ballet. He was the director, choreographer, and protagonist of *Don Quixote*. Dance, his natural element, became a field to be explored with every possible means.

There was also the Nureyev of the small screen. Joking and in search of the sympathy of the vast American audience, he took part in a self-deprecating parody of *Swan Lake*. A guest on the *Muppet Show*, he danced with an enormous foam-rubber pig, Miss Piggy. The improbable *pas de deux* concludes with the swan-pig being thrown unceremoniously off the stage. Not in the least discouraged, she comes back to her prince.

A visionary director, however, was responsible for the real consecration of Nureyev in the cinema. Ken Russell was provocative and in tune with the Flying Tartar. His film *Valentino* was made in 1977. It starts with the sumptuous funeral (strangely prophetic of Nureyev's funeral in January 1993) of this immigrant Italian dancer-gigolo who becomes a Hollywood myth. There are three dancers in the film: Leslie Caron plays the Lesbian Nazimova, Lindsay Kemp the funeral director, and Anthony Dowell, in the part of Vaslav Nijinski as he dances a pas de deux with Nureyev/Valentino.

After Russell's *Valentino*, there was also an attempt to launch Nureyev into the star system in *Exposed*. A very young Nastassja Kinski was his co-star. The film went almost unnoticed. The protocols and the long time frames of movie-making were incompatible with what was, for Nureyev, first and foremost his dancing. He did try, however, in his *Cinderella*, to combine these two worlds, by giving this fable a Hollywood interpretation.

In 1981 he was cast as the shy, bespectacled teacher in a children's film for television. It was directed by Mario Lanfranchi and shot on the canals of Venice. Carla Fracci was Nureyev's partner and the narrator was Peter Ustinov. It was called *Carnevale a Venezia* and was dedicated to saving the artistic heritage of that city.

In 1981 Nureyev appeared as the lead in the French film for television, *Coup de Foudre*. His experience in the musical *The King and I*, by Rogers and Hammerstein, in 1989 proved that he was extremely versatile. It also underlined the fact that he belonged to the stage. It must be said, however, that Nureyev was also attracted by the musical because he could be on stage without greatly exerting himself. He was required to play a king who learns to dance, quite a paradox for him, and this suited him as his illness was becoming daily more demanding.

Mario Monicelli had an idea to cast him as an old Beethoven. Nureyev was attracted to the project in his last years. His appearance was more ethereal, and he was ever more engaged in making a superhuman effort toward "high" music. To him this was a dimension in which all the arts converged to the highest point of his tempestuous life.

The Flying Tartar's Experiments in Europe and New York

A Lucifer with a sculpted body, the lion's mane, the flying cloak open like diabolical wings, a band across his forehead that makes him look like a pirate. But he is the damned and fallen angel, half-man, half-god. Proud, ferocious. He balances on a stylized sculpture by Isamu Moguchi. This is Nureyev as seen by Martha Graham, the pioneer of modern dance. In 1975 she created *Lucifer* for him. The music was by El-Dabh. Beneath Graham's severe

gaze, the arrogant prince bowed, almost to extinction, as he became a participant of one of the great diktats of modern dance. The real artist sacrifices all his narcissism, his boundless personality, to absolute simplicity. Thus began for Nureyev, on the one hand, a process of paring down his technical grammar to remove the tinsel from his nineteenth-century tradition. On the other hand, there began a process of introspection into interpretative research. He left behind the leaps, the elevation, the upward thrust of classical ballet. Now he was to discover grounding. He studied the contraction-release mechanism, the anchoring of movement to the most visceral part of the body—the hips, the famous backward falls.

Classical and modern have in common a devotion to dance. In her autobiography *Blood Memory* Martha Graham described Nureyev as a god of light, to whom she had entrusted her Lucifer, literally meaning "he who brings light." She dedicated to him William Blake's "Tiger! tiger! burning bright / In the forests of the night . . ."

Nureyev was interested in modern dance from the day he arrived in the West; from the day at Maude Gosling's house in Richmond Park when he saw a film about the Martha Graham Dance Company. "I must learn it," he said. In Vienna, he later created a *Tancredi* to music by Henze. It was saturated with lessons that he had learned from Graham, from Paul Taylor, from Glen Tetley.

When Martha Graham and her company brought *Night Journey* on tour to London, Nureyev had only recently defected. With Maude and Nigel Gosling he went backstage after the performance. Rudolf was so overcome that he stared at Martha Graham and did not speak.

Nureyev also dragged Margot Fonteyn into the adventure of *Lucifer*. She insisted on dancing barefoot, although Martha Graham did not agree. At first the two stars frightened Graham. "They were the incarnation of the ideal of ballet," she wrote in her autobiography, "and instead [. . .] it was so easy to work with them. They were extremely reactive artists, passionate, and their ability to confront new techniques was very moving." Of Graham's ballets, Nureyev danced *El penitente*; *The Scarlet Letter*, composed for him; *Night Journey*; *Appalachian Spring* with Baryshnikov, with Micha in the role of the Groom and Rudolf in that of the Preacher. Nureyev, Fonteyn, and Baryshnikov performed free for a season with the Martha Graham Company. Martha Graham even confessed "What I would have given to be able to dance with Rudolf."

But the Graham school was only one of the experiments that Nureyev tried in the United States. His incursions into modern and contemporary dance included Paul Taylor. Nureyev danced Taylor's *Aureole* in 1971. It was filmed in 1978 with Vivi Flindt, Eva Klobor, and Anne Sonnerup. Nureyev appreciated Taylor's

ability to invent original steps, structures never seen before, and surprising contortions. In 1971, dressed in a curious chimpanzee costume, he had already danced in Taylor's *A Book of Beasts*, inspired by Borges. At the other end of the line of modern dance was José Limòn. Nureyev danced his *The Moor's Pavane*, to music by Purcell, for the first time in 1972. This was a *pas de quatre* of jealousy and death with Othello, Iago, Desdemona, and Emilia, and was one of the pieces that Nureyev was to insert into his "evenings" with Friends, right until the end.

The most important encounter in New York, however, was that with the master of neo-classicism, George Balanchine. He was the unsurpassed inventor of abstract architecture, using the dancers as instruments in a higher design. Balanchine had also come from the Kirov in Leningrad. When Nureyev asked if he could join his company, The New York City Ballet, Balanchine discouraged him. "My choreography is dry, no stars. Get rid of your princes and come back." In 1967 Nureyev became the most ardent *Apollo* that had ever come out of Balanchine's mind. In 1972 he danced his *Prodigal Son*, and *Agon* in 1973. Sixteen years later they worked together on *Le Bourgeois gentilhomme*. The dancer was fascinated by the way of creating choreography, from the beginning of the score to the end, following the intensity of the scales.

In America, Nureyev also worked with Jerome Robbins. In 1971 he danced his *Afternoon of a Faun*. It was a contemporary and stylized version of Nijinski's *Après-midi d'un Faune* (1912). Before that, Nureyev had appeared in *Dances at a Gathering* in 1969. He danced Murray Louis's abstract *Moment*, to music by Ravel.

In 1970, with the American choreographer Glen Tetley, he experimented with the exploration of space through sequences of movement that were inspired by animals in *Field Figures*, set to electronic music by Karlheinz Stockhausen. In partnership with Deanne Bergsma, he developed positions, subjugations, and contortions in a relationship of confrontation and tension in which the two dancers interacted intimately, imitating birds, serpents, and monkeys. It was something that, over time, man has subconsciously put into motion, like an ancestral heritage of animal defense. In 1971, he took on *Laborintus* by the same author, with music by Luciano Berio, about life as an inextricable and infernal labyrinth. Nureyev also played the poetic and agonizing *Pierrot Lunaire*. In white lead makeup, he would hang from a metal scaffolding-sculpture designed by Ter-Arutunian, and with music by Schonberg. Like Pierrot, Nureyev played in his tower with moonbeams.

In 1974, he danced *Tristan* with Carolyn Carlson, Tetley's reflection of the Wagnerian opera *Tristan und Isolde*.

Maurice Béjart made him a gift of a ballet that he was to dance until the end. *Chant du Compagnon Errant* was a *pas de deux* with a mysterious alter-ego that represents fate, death. Created for him and Paolo Bortoluzzi in 1970, it was interpreted by Nureyev in parallel with the choral *Sacre du Printemps*, which was the masterpiece of the maestro from Marseilles.

With these choreographies Nureyev was focused on an essential part of his vision of dance. "There are many interesting characters," he explained, "but what counts is to show the emotions, the state of mind, the mood. This way the character becomes abstract. Choreographers like Robbins, Balanchine, Martha Graham are moving in this direction. And this is also my idea of what the dance should be."

Paris: Triumph and Power

In Paris, Nureyev had himself portrayed as the muse Tersicore that appears in a dominating position on the roof of the Opéra Garnier. It testifies that here, at the Palais, designed by Charles Garnier for Napoleon III, ballet is king. It was very different to La Scala, where the dance was and is, by tradition and nineteenth century cultural inheritance, the handmaiden of melodrama.

The Palais Garnier could not have been a better place for Nureyev to celebrate the consecration of his personal power after years of peregrinations as a guest star. It was a way to take stock and at last see the sum of his choreographic work in an organic whole.

His artistic path in the West began in Paris. In Paris he was to deliver the last of his visions, a *Bayadère* of sumptuous beauty. In Paris he had enlarged and cemented his cultural horizons, with a close encounter with Roland Petit, the first choreographer who had noticed him. Petit had challenged him with his existential and extremely refined ballets. The first, in 1966, was *Paradise Lost*, a transposition in dance of the fall of Adam and Eve, with Margot Fonteyn in the role, with the Royal Ballet. With Zizi Jeanmaire, *Le Jeune Homme et la Mort* came the same year, in a film for television. It is the story of a poet who commits suicide for love and discovers at the end that the woman for whom he has lost himself is Death. Two years later it was the turn of *L'estasi*, with sets by De Chirico, and *Pelléas et Melisande*, with Margot Fonteyn and the Royal Ballet. Petit gave him advice and criticism when he was installed as director of the Ballet de l'Opéra de Paris in 1982.

After the departure of Rolf Lieberman in 1979, the Opéra was going through a profoundly critical period. There were internal crises, partly genetic to the nature of any great institution, but also *vis à vis* the public. The Opéra seemed to be unable to entice the new generation with proposals for change. Jack Lang, then the Minister of Culture, aimed at bringing the Opéra back to its old splendor by attracting a new audience. Lang counted on Nureyev to shake up public opinion. His name was the most popular and the most provocative in dance. Later he said, "I considered Nureyev a sort of unreachable, supernatural divinity, and I was not sure that he would accept my proposal."

Some people compared the arrival of Nureyev at the Opéra to the Normandy landings. Beyond the emphatic tone of the parallel, it is certain that the arrival of the Russian in Paris shook even the foundations of the bureaucratic apparatus of the Opéra and the status of the ballet company. The company was in search of that pride that every evening, on the stage, is generally called the *grandeur parisienne*. At last, the Company had found its identity in Nureyev.

Massimo Bogiankino was named general manager of the Opéra; André Larquié was the president. Soviet resistance was overcome by the personal intervention of François Mitterrand. Perplexity as to the notoriously tempestuous dancer was also overcome. The assignment was made. Among the conditions that Nureyev insisted upon were a free hand, both financially in the dance as separate from the opera, and artistically in the choice of the repertory, distribution, and the professors and ballet masters. He also asked for the guarantee of a certain number of performances of the ballet both at home and on tour. It was Nureyev who requested that the great cupola over the theatre, likened to an enormous wedding cake, be hollowed out to make room for three rehearsal rooms. And, according to André Larquié, who became president of the Circle of Friends of Nureyev, it was Nureyev who suggested that the Palais Garnier be dedicated to dance when the Opéra Bastille was opened. By contract, Nureyev was allowed to be absent for six months a year in order to pursue his activities as a freelance professional of dance. But what he most cared about was to discover and launch new talent and expand the repertory of the company.

It opened his first season as director, with the whole company on stage in *Raymonda*. His prime objective was to put a whole generation of twenty year olds in the spotlight. He promoted Sylvie Guillem, Isabelle Guerin, Laurent Hilaire, and Elisabeth Maurin.

His second objective brought the arrival at the Opéra of John Neumeier, William Forsythe, Maurice Béjart, Maguy Marin, Twyla Tharp, Merce Cunningham, Jerome Robbins, Lucinda Childs, Louis Falco, Rudy Van Dantzig, Dominique Bagouet, Francine Lancelot, David Parsons, and Daniel Ezralow. He commissioned *Le Martyre de Saint Sébastien* from Bob Wilson. It had its debut on 23 March 1988 with Sylvie Guillem, Michael Denard, Patrick Dupond, and the performers Philippe Chemin and Sheryl Sutton. At Nureyev's insistence forgotten repertory was explored, such as *Arlequin, magicien par amour* and the *Dansomanie*, reconstructed by Ivo Cramer. The baroque patrimony was re-evaluated with the choreography of Francine Lancelot for *Bach Suite* and *Quelque pas graves de Baptiste*.

After thirty years of absence, in 1986, the Ballet de l'Opéra performed before the public of the Metropolitan. The young dancers were scintillating. Even though his presence was a shining example for dancers, Nureyev never wanted to create clones. He would say of them, "They are extraordinary, better than me and those who went before me. Their technique is clearer and more refined. And as far as interpretation is concerned, they are like great musicians. They can interpret anything from Mozart to Beethoven, to Schönberg to Stockhausen. This is the coming generation."

In conclusion, during the eight years of Nureyev's direction, the Company underwent a profound change, the effects of which were to last a long time, even though his tenure was characterized by many heated arguments like that with Béjart for the promotion to *étoile* of Eric Vu An. After his departure, the ballet put on performances chosen by him, like *Sacre de Printemps* by Nijinsky and *Dances at a Gathering* by Jerome Robbins. Since then the Parisian company has maintained its world supremacy.

Nureyev bought a house in Paris, where he probably spent most of his time. It was an apartment at Twenty-three Quai Voltaire, and the decoration was entrusted to Emilio Carcano, a *protégé* of Renzo Mongiardino, the Italian architect who, in 1967, had designed the sets for *Nutcracker* for the Royal Swedish Ballet of Stockholm. Carcano designed the house sumptuously and transformed it into a home fit for a king, a symbol of the power and wealth accumulated by Nureyev, collector of antiques.

"Where there's a will there's a way," Rudolf maintained. But power turned its back on him and did not want him anymore. His voyage in the temple of French culture concluded in 1989. His contract was not renewed and Nureyev found himself ousted from his position as director of the Ballet de l'Opéra, even though the significance of that adventure was recognized by France. In 1988, the Légion d'Honneur was presented to him by President François Mitterand.

Italy and the Broken Dream of Li Galli

Three rocky islands of Mediterranean scrub survey the bay of Positano. They are Il Gallo Lungo, la Rotonda, and Castelluccio. This is the tiny archipelago called Li Galli that the Roman historian Strabone indicated as the "land of the sirens" of Ulysses, put into verse by Homer. In the forties, it was the remote reign of a great Russian of the dance world, the choreographer Leonide Massine, who had extravagantly made himself part of the life of Positano, bringing with him a court of admirers. In ancient times the islands were baptised Li Galli from the Phoenician for "gaulos," the mercantile ships that sailed those seas. In 1988 that island of dance passed into the hands of Nureyev, another Russian.

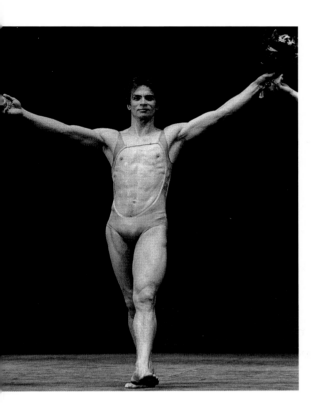

Rudolf had discovered it some years earlier when he had gone there to receive a prize. He fell hopelessly in love. He decided to add it to the other properties that he possessed all over the world. Nureyev had a special relationship with his homes. Even though he was absent most of the time (he spent very little time in any of his homes), from a distance, he had a profound nostalgia for each of them. He thought he would enjoy them later, when his age would have forced him into a more sedentary way of life.

His first home was at La Turbie, on the hills overlooking Monte Carlo. It was a villa built on one floor. It had belonged to an opera singer who used to go there to practice undisturbed. There was a bedroom, a living room, and a bathroom. It was surrounded by a military area, therefore off-limits and perfect for Nureyev's desire for isolation. When a highway was built below the house, Rudolf decided to sell. The London house, at Richmond Park, was also shielded from observation and protected from curious eyes. With his increasing wealth, Nureyev added other properties in the following years: the Paris apartment in Quai Voltaire; the farm in Leesburg Virginia; the house at Saint-Barthélemy in the Caribbean; and the New York apartment at the Dakota on Central Park West. This was entrusted to the Italian architect Emilio Carcano and to the British decorator Tessa Kennedy. It was transformed into a princely residence in the seventeenth-century European baroque style.

When Nureyev was asked what a house meant to him, he would reply, "It is the place where there is somebody waiting for you. For me home is the theatre. The public is there and waiting for me." Maybe it was in order to put together the fragments of a private life that Nureyev had ended by collecting houses that were crammed with works of art. From the rocks of Li Galli he could see the sea. Usually naked, he would plough through the waves on his water scooter, often irritated by the curiosity of tourists. Massine's old custodian, Giovanni, lived there all the year round. Il Gallo Lungo, the biggest of the islands, had a heliport and a lighthouse. There was a four-story Saracen tower, divided into nine rooms and five bathrooms covered with antique Turkish *azuléjos* and a gym where Nureyev would exercise every day. It was here that Rudolf dreamed of having a school for the young talent that would survive him.

The last time he went to the island, on 3 September 1992, he kissed the rocks before leaving, knowing that he would not return. What he did not imagine, however, was that his dream would also die with him. After a series of offers by local corporations, during which the island was bounced between the Comune of Positano, which wanted to transform it into a museum, and the Campania Region, the island was put up for sale by a foundation in Nureyev's name. It was bought by four local businessmen. Franco Zeffirelli

and Carla Fracci vainly appealed for the property not to be transferred. Ten years after the death of Nureyev, the destiny of Li Galli seems to have been decided: it is not a dance school but a luxury hotel.

Music and the Illness

Nureyev used to say, talking about "his" music: Tchiakovsky is the Father, Prokofiev the Son, Stravinsky the Holy Spirit. In the center of this Holy Trinity, embedded in the most Russian of the scores of the last century, Nureyev hoped to find his alternative to glory, the refuge from the insidiousness of the illness that had struck him down, sapping his strength every time he went on stage. To conduct an orchestra: the Maestro's baton could become a magic wand, giving him safe conduct to eternity. So it was that Nureyev faced his last Prokofiev by conducting a *Romeo and Juliet* from the orchestra pit at the Metropolitan. The dancers were Sylvie Guillem and Laurent Hilaire. He had known Stravinsky personally, and had conducted his *Apollon Musagète* at a concert in Deauville. He had tackled Tchaikovsky with the Wiener Residenz Orchester. He had chosen the *Serenata for String Orchestra in C major, op. 48*, followed by the *Symphony in D major Hob. 73, The Hunt* by Haydn, and the *Concerto for Violin and Orchestra in D major n. 4 KV218* by Mozart. Fearless as he was, for a conductor with such little experience, he had to attempt the impossible. He conducted Beethoven's *Third Symphony* in Vienna with a youth orchestra. He had decided, at the age of forty-nine, to begin studying piano. He thought that, while he was director of the Ballet de l'Opéra de Paris, he had better learn something. He had always loved music. Before going out to face a performance he would often listen to a recording of Bach.

It was the conductor Herbert von Karajan, his neighbor at the Dakota in New York, who advised him to take up the baton. "You should become a conductor. Conductors live a long life. I will give you private lessons and I'll teach you the secrets of the job." But it was impossible for these two very busy people to get together. Karajan's words remained just an anecdote, but they were prophetic. From that time on Rudolf asked for a clause in his contract that, wherever possible, he be supplied with a piano in his hotel room and one in his dressing room. He had lived in symbiosis with music for thirty-seven years. Now he just took the next step. He had to deal with the music itself now, without the mediation of movement. He used to say, "Even Bernstein jumped around on the podium like a dancer."

In 1991, at the end of a concert he gave in Ravello, he said in a television interview, "I have had this idea for years. I was just waiting for the moment. There is a professor in Vienna, Wilhelm

Hübner, who has been saying for ten years that I should become a conductor. He phoned me a couple of months ago to tell me that I could have fifteen rehearsals with the orchestra in Vienna. I accepted." Hübner was a violinist of high regard. He prepared Nureyev for the concert he held under the enormous vault of the Auersperg Palais in Vienna, in the hall dedicated to music. Nureyev called him "Papà Hübner" and followed his instructions with filial respect. He would peer seriously at the score and shoot glances at his young players. He had begun by playing Bach on the piano, slowly, to study the secrets of the preludes and fugues. He chose to celebrate the evening of the thirtieth anniversary of his defection to the West, in the company of the Hubner family, Wilhelm, his wife Lidia and their daughter. After Vienna came the concert in Ravello, then another in Varese at the Teatro Impero. He had more concerts in his schedule, during which he would have conducted Beethoven, and Mozart again. The press treated his new career as though it was a news item, not much more than a curiosity in the calendar of events. Some insinuated that this change signaled Nureyev's farewell to the stage. Very few realized the human drama that was hidden behind that choice.

When he was young, Rudolf hoped that he would die in his bed, a very old man. Later he tenaciously insisted, "I must go on dancing to the last breath." When, in his youth, they asked him what his plans were for his old age, he would reply, "I try to move in various directions; there is much to discover in the stage, acting, teaching. For the time being I am dancing, and well. It is quite natural that I should try to do it as long as possible." As the years passed, he adapted to the changes in his body, saying "I cannot compete with myself, like I was yesterday. But today there is a special quality in my dancing that I have distilled over time and it is the fruit of a life of study and sacrifice. Dance is what I am, yesterday as today."

Possibly he deceived himself that he would become a grand old man of dance, a patriarch to whom everybody would come for advice. The illness bowed him, but it took more than ten years. He never wanted to say the word AIDS, and as a mark of respect, nobody in his circle ever did either. Brief signals, understanding looks, the illusion that at least his own wrestler's body would win. His doctor was Michel Canesi, who later said, "We knew very little about the illness at that time. We thought that only 10 percent of HIV positive people developed the disease. So it didn't seem that serious." When the disease became evident, apprehension and concern began to spread among the dancers at the Opéra. His muscles dried up, and his expressive face suddenly became gaunt. He was on tour in the United States with *The King and I* in 1989. The producers became alarmed and asked him to take some clinical tests for insurance purposes. At first he put it off, then he had a doctor friend send a certificate of good health. The illness came and went, alternating times when the body seemed to snuff out, to times when it would miraculously revive. He kept control right to the end. Dance still expected him.

The Last *Bayadère*: the Curtain Falls

The Kingdom of Shades. This was how Nureyev chose his farewell to his public, with the mythical image of thirty-two fantastic creatures dressed in tutùs, vestals of the afterlife embodied in *A Thousand and One Nights*. Nikiya, la Bayadère, the Dancing Girl, has been bitten by the asp prepared by the perfidious Princess Gamzatti. The desperate Solor rushes to her side, but she is already beyond the land of the living. This is the story of a warrior who looks for the reason for his human and fallible destiny in expiation. It is not unlike the action of the noble, faithless, penitent, and troubled Albrecht in the second act of *Giselle*. It is a farewell between two worlds. One is the earthly, scintillating, and exotic world; the other is the Afterlife, insubstantial and mysterious. Separated for eternity. After the years of his direction of the Opéra, he regretted not having mounted *La Bayadère*, which had been the first ballet that he had appeared in, in Paris in 1961. The Opéra granted his wish when they saw how ill he was.

Seated in the stalls, dressed in heavy sweaters, he would watch the company rehearse, making small gestures with ever paler hands, but still alive and attentive.

It was due to his iron will that the dancers were able to perform a miracle and mount the three-act ballet in only three weeks. It was the titanic undertaking of a heroic man. His wish was to live his fidelity to dance right up to his martyrdom. On the evening of the first performance, 8 October 1992, the Opéra was pervaded by the sublime and moving atmosphere of a special evening. Nureyev watched the performance from a box to the left of the stage. He was almost at the end of his strength and was assisted by his doctor, Michel Canesi. During the intervals, lines of friends and acquaintances went to pay their respects. It was a triumph. At the end of the performance, he decided that this time he would go and salute his public.

"I have to do it!" he said. "But let's do it quickly." With great difficulty and helped along, he reached the stage. The audience realized that this was a farewell. He was a shadow among his Shadows dressed in costume. There were fifteen seconds of complete silence, then the applause began. And, summoning up all his strength, Nureyev straightened up to make his last bow. His dancers crowded round him and sat him down. Jack Lang presented him with an award and made a brief speech. The television cameras revealed the signs of illness in his face, and his imminent end. Thus ended Nureyev's long voyage on the world scene.

The days following were sad and grey. He was admitted under a false name to the Hospital Pérpetuel Secours at Levallois-Perret, in Room 517, until the first days of December. Then he returned, with the help of friends, to the five rooms on Quai Voltaire overlooking the Seine. The press laid siege to the apartment, but the newspapers had already announced the devastation of the illness in headlines after the premiere of *Bayadère*. Nureyev made plans right up to the end: *Nutcracker, Sleeping Beauty, Romeo and Juliet* . . . He died at 3:30 in the afternoon on 6 January 1993, Christmas Day in Russia. Rudolf slipped away in his sleep, surrounded by his longtime friends. Paris prepared her farewell with three days of mourning, during which a lavish funeral was arranged. It was celebrated in three acts. On January 11, people filed past a giant photograph of Nureyev in the columned porch of the Opéra. On January 12 the art world and official Paris took part in the wake. At his lying in state politicians lined up and Minister Jack Lang gave the funeral oration: "Astronomers say that the light of certain stars shines for a long time after they themselves have disappeared." The ceremony was concluded at Sainte-Geneviève-des-Bois. Many Russian émigrés who had escaped during the Bolshevic revolution were buried in this cemetery, where Nureyev was laid to rest. Ezio Frigerio, one of Nureyev's favorite set designers, designed a tomb stone. It is a sculpture that the Flying Tartar would have liked—a traveling bag, in oriental tapestry, made in mosaic glass from Murano.

The world press gave ample space to the death of Nureyev. Only the Soviet press, still mindful of ancient grudges, ignored the news. The official Russian press organ, *Itar-Tass*, dealt with it in a few lines, in an anonymous headline: "A famous dancer dies." Not even with perestroika had Russia forgiven the "traitor to the nation." Russian dance rendered homage to its most illustrious son. On 8 January, *Le Figaro* published an interview with Oleg Vinogradov, the director of the Kirov. The headline was "*Un tel artiste devait danser pour la terre entière*" (Such an artist must dance for the whole world). And so the most dazzling talent that dance has ever know, vanished.

What is left? His immense fortune was divided between two foundations in his name, and among his close relations. Time has delivered to the public the lesson of an artist who embodied dance and rendered it human, divine, and emotionally vibrant.

Nureyev's Legacy

There is no point in asking if there are any heirs to Nureyev today. It was his uniqueness that made him. An outstanding talent cannot be substituted. Nureyev will always be irreplaceable.

Nureyev placed himself as a bridge between two cultures, the Russian and the American, by mediation of the English and French. He was himself an exceptional communicator, both in the real and the metaphorical sense. He could probably be described as the first dancer of the media. He had tasted the power of television. This was the medium that in 1960, a year before his defection, had played a fundamental role in the election of the American president, John F. Kennedy. Nureyev arrived at the precise historical moment in communication that changed the relationship between scenic vision and information. He was the ballet star elected by the global village of television. From that moment on, even the other refugees, like Natalia Makarova and Michail Baryshnikov, found their own special places in the information age and in the minds of the public.

Technically, Nureyev raised the standards of western ballet. Not only in the interpretation of the male roles, but also in the manner of being the partner, no longer a support, a mere partner for the ballerina, but a star in his own right. His ability to put his partners into the spotlight was amply recognized by them.

Before Nureyev it was very hard to find a poster of a male dancer. The absolute star was the ballerina, a throwback to a supremacy that had come into being in the nineteenth century with Romanticism. There are exceptions in the history of dance, like Vaslav Nijinski, who marked the first twenty years of the twentieth century with Diaghilev's Ballets Russes, or much earlier, in the eighteenth century, the French Vestris, Gaetano, the father, and August, the son. They were formidable dancers in a legendary family of Italian origin, *premiers danseurs* of the Ballet de l'Opéra and pupils of Jean-Georges Noverre, whose arrival in London in 1781 caused such a sensation that Parliament interrupted their sessions to coincide with their performances.

Even for the public that did not usually follow the ballet, Nureyev is associated with the idea of dance like Rodolfo Valentino represented silent film. This was a parallel that Ken Russell certainly did not miss when he asked the dancer to play the part of his *Valentino*.

On stage, Nureyev profoundly changed the way of communicating with the audience. He catalyzed it, imposing himself and changing the relationship between "being" and "giving of himself" on the stage. His cat-like walk toward the proscenium, opening his arms and bowing low to receive the applause, encircling the public in an ideal embrace, was copied by almost everyone. He was a master in maneuvering excessively long cloaks, enveloping, bewitching, and pulsating with passion and mystery. Nureyev was a champion of the rite of the curtain call. The record of eighty-nine calls for him and Margot Fonteyn at the Opera Theatre in Vienna in October 1964 at the end of *Swan Lake* has never been surpassed.

And so the moment of applause became an art. It was no longer a sign of public appreciation, but the ideal continuation of the performance, as though it were the coda, an extract where emotions were concentrated and then liberated by the clapping hands of the spectators. In ballet class, lessons were learned in how to enter and exit the stage. It was a habit that was soon imitated by the young dancers of the Royal Ballet.

In terms of the market of show business, Nureyev revolutionized the fees for dancers. In part, he filled the gap that separated the star of the ballet from that of the golden voices of opera. With him, arrogance became a quality of the prince who upset all the co-ordinates of the *danseur noble*. His passport to enter into the hearts of the public was his complete adherence to the character. It was a quality that his friend and rival, Michail Baryshnikov, recognized after his death: "He had the charisma and simplicity of a man of the earth and the untouchable arrogance of the gods."

Nureyev treated the ballet with all the respect it deserved. It was serious and not just a pretty entertainment for children, for aspiring ex-dancers, or groups of tourists. He was like the theater director Giorgio Strehler, who detested theatre for "the child," but was in favor of a theatre for "little men." Nureyev approached fable with discipline. His first complete ballet in the West was exemplary. It was *Nutcracker*. He dismissed the childlike readings of the melodrama of Christmas. Instead, he embraced a vision of a completely different dramatic weight. It was to be a voyage of initiation into the mysteries of dreams and life.

Even though Nureyev danced beyond his own physical limits, he insisted that dance should be young. He launched a whole generation of twenty-year-old stars and demonstrated to the ancient world of ballet that even traditional organizations like the Opéra should dismantle the old rules of professional advancement. And he left to the young ballet directors an example that still shines.

It is curious to note how many companies he danced with. In his very busy schedules, besides institutions like La Scala and the Royal Ballet, were foreign companies beyond the great circuits, like the Ballet of the Teatro Colón in Buenos Aires, the Norwegian Ballet, or small companies like the Niagara Frontier Ballet and the Wisconsin Ballet. With the innumerable tours of the Friends, Nureyev put into operation a capillary system of divulgement of dance. He brought his shows to disenfranchised places, to outdoor summer stages set up under the stars, to villas and arenas. In the calendar of his tours in 1986 there is even a *Giselle* in the Seychelles.

In a career that has no equal, Nureyev put into practice what, for Béjart, was a commandment: "Ballet is an art of the twentieth century."

Nureyev, the Image

In Ralph Fassey's photographs you will not see a Nureyev who made history through the decades, but his quintessence, the abstraction from time and space. We will see "our" Nureyev. The Nureyev who, in Murray Louis's *Moment*, breaks the pure and perfect lines of the Kirov by which he was formed, to show a body that was honed by his encounters with Martha Graham, George Balanchine, Jerome Robbins, Maurice Béjart, and Glen Tetley. He is Apollo meeting Dionysus. He has learned the lesson of evolution through the most ardent of passion and the discovery of the freedom of his body. A vibrant body and, therefore, intelligent, and the powerful instrument of an omnivorous mind and a free spirit.

This Nureyev was cut down at the height of his maturity and at his human and artistic peak. He left us an unsurpassed lesson of the intelligence of dance, far away from any cultural ghettos. This is a Nureyev who knows how to pass through dance, scanning all its grammar, from the virtuosity of the Czarist academy to the expressive elegance of the English style, to modern dance of Martha Graham, the anthropomorphic experiments of Glenn Tetley, and the superhuman dance of Béjart. This is a prophetic Nureyev delivering us a ballet that is cultivated and aware of its own capability, ready to accept the challenges of the new millennium.

Photographing Nureyev

by Ralph Fassey

Those who have had the good fortune of seeing Nureyev in the flesh have had to bow to the rules of the great theatrical tradition: he on the stage, they in the audience.

I have been one of those lucky people, but I have had a fate that was less severe, a destiny that was far too generous.

My first, and completely chance, meeting with Rudolf was both improbable and unbelievable, and it defined all our successive meetings. This book is a witness.

That evening, Nureyev was not performing. He was just a lone spectator, sitting some rows in front of me at the Palais des Congrès in Paris. It was a great surprise, and what brought us to that place that evening was an even greater surprise. It was not a ballet, not a concert, but a long contemporary meditation on the theme of prayer. It was *Inori*, a work for orchestra and dancer-mimes, directed by Karlheinz Stockhausen, the composer himself.

There was just the time to catch a picture of that unexpected spectator with my camera, and then I approached him. I had only ever seen him in video or photographs. He could have refused me, considering me an unwelcome intruder. But he greeted me calmly and simply… he was even slightly curious. I had with me a work on *Stimmung* that Stockhausen had commissioned from me, and that I was to deliver to him after the performance. Without going into banal eulogies and endless discourses about the dance, I showed him my work. Nureyev took it and began to turn the pages with interest.

And so an unusual and personal relationship was born. It was not based on the admiration of a fan nor a professional rapport or friendship. I just had a great thirst to know and understand Nureyev, and all the moments that had marked his life.

I was quickly accepted into the circle of people who went backstage to talk to him after a performance, and often even before he went on stage. Every time, I would show him the latest photographs of Stockhausen's concerts, for example, the memorable performances of Sirius at Saint-Chapelle in Paris, or of Inori at the Hérode Atticus theatre in Athens.

His interest was lively and intense. From his questions, it seemed to me that he was a great professional, conscious of the importance of detail and sensitive to the practical difficulties of mounting a performance.

So it was that, every time Nureyev performed in Paris, either at the Palais Garnier, the Palais des Sports or the Palais des Congrès, I was able to observe him closely during all the years of his glittering artistry. He was a star in the most profound meaning of the word. He was, in fact, a man of incredible depth and wealth of spirit. He was a real Tartar in the way that he could reveal a great range of temperament in one single instant.

I still have many memories of these encounters, and they are all incredibly alive in my mind. There are thousands of photographs. Never published. A sort of iconographic *Sleeping Beauty…*

This book represents a selection of unpublished images not just to remember the great Nureyev as the world remembers and loves him, the actor, the dancer, the artist. Above all it intends to show him detached from the usual clichés, and how it was possible to know him far away from the splendor and magnificence and the spotlights. A different Nureyev.

I was able to know this Nureyev and catch him in moments of solitude, during the pre-rehearsals that nobody was allowed to attend, in his dressing room as he put on his makeup, intensely concentrated, or after the performance, calm and relaxed. All the phases of his day as a dancer and that gravitated around the performance, the key moment of his life. They were simply a moment of preparation or a moment of recreation. It was those moments, however, that revealed the man Nureyev, and sometimes even the child Nureyev, and that were the most intense.

Ten years after his death, among thousands of official images that the whole world offers of him, the publication of these photographs tries to bring to life a more human Rudolf, and in consequence, ever more present.

Milan, 6 January 2003

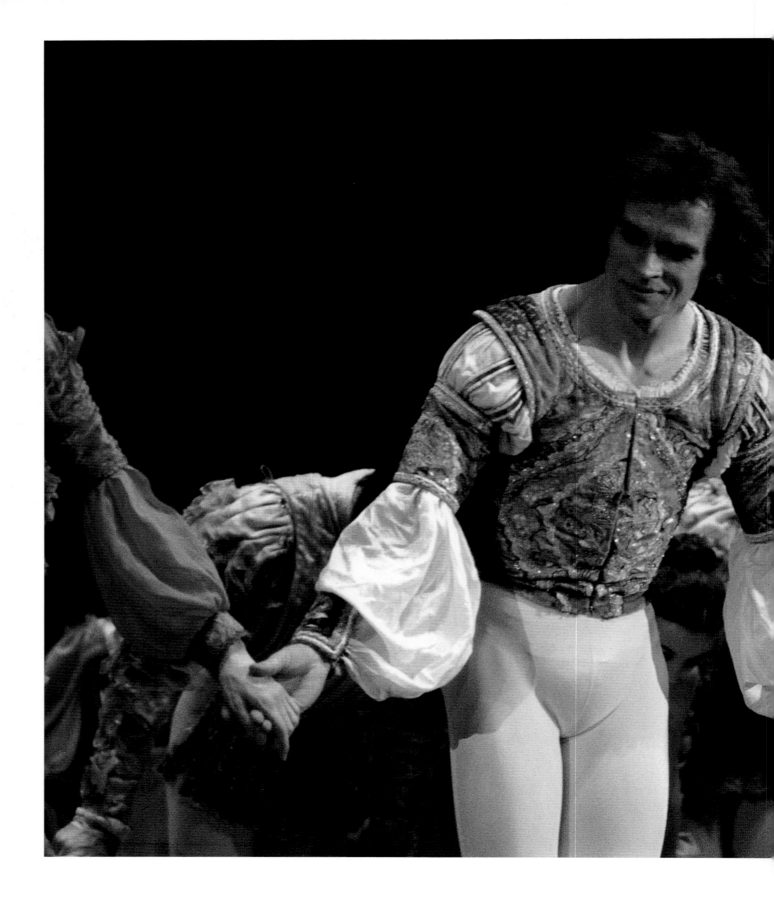

83

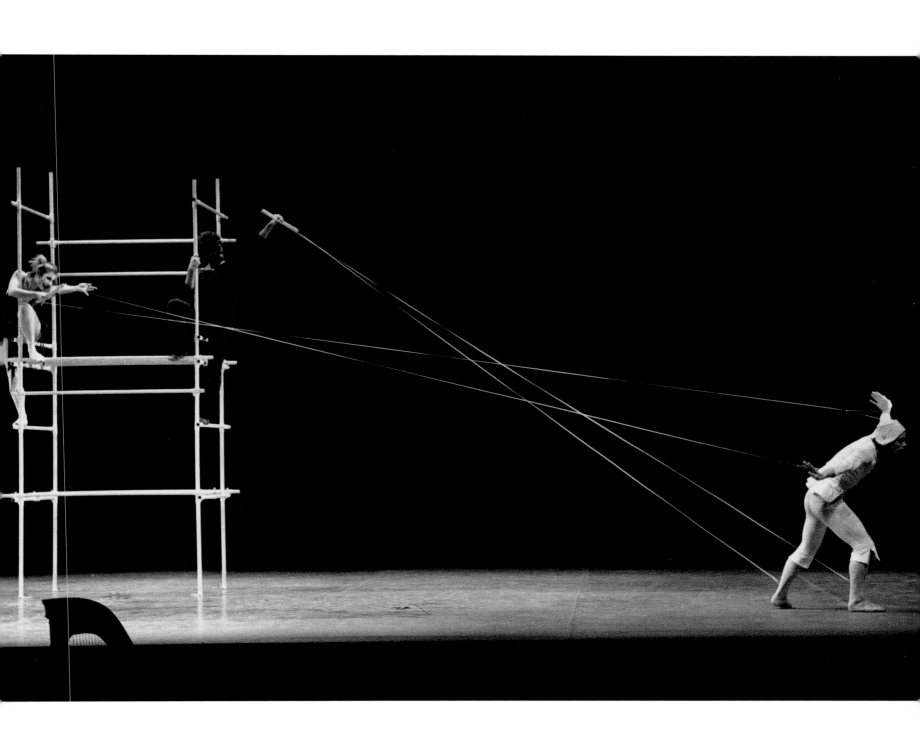

64
Giselle, *Scottish Ballet,*
February 1977,
Palais des Sports, Paris

66–79
Romeo and Juliet, *Festival*
Ballet with Patricia Ruanne,
January 1978, Palais des
Sports, Paris

80–85
Chant du Compagnon
Errant, *February,*
Palais des Sports, Paris

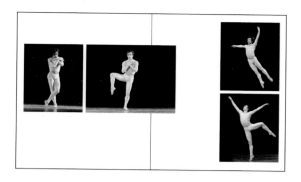

86–101
Swan Lake, *Ballet de l'Opéra
de Paris with Ghislaine
Thesmar, March 1980, Palais
des Congrès, Paris*

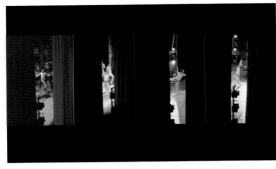

102–103
Rehearsals for Four
Schumann Pieces

104–107
Four Schumann Pieces,
National Ballet of Canada,
February 1977, Palais des
Sports, Paris

108–111
La Sylphide, *Scottish Ballet*
with Natalia Makarova,
February 1977, Palais des
Sports, Paris

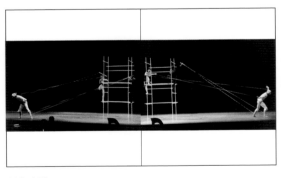

112–119
Pierrot Lunaire, *with Vivi*
Flindt and Johnny Eliasen,
February 1977, Palais des
Sports, Paris

120–125
Sleeping Beauty, *Ballet Théâtre de Nancy with Wilfride Piollet, April 1983, Palais des Congrès, Paris*

126–129
Sleeping Beauty, *Festival Ballet with Patricia Ruanne, January 1976, Palais des Sports, Paris*

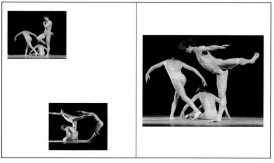

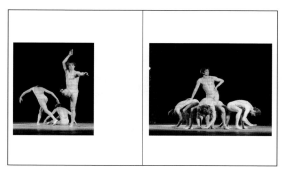

130–141
Moment, *Scottish Ballet, February 1977, Palais des Sports, Paris*

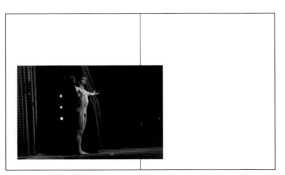

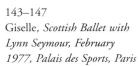

143–147
Giselle, *Scottish Ballet with
Lynn Seymour, February
1977, Palais des Sports, Paris*

148–149
Four Schumann Pieces,
*National Ballet of Canada,
February 1977, Palais des
Sports, Paris*

154

Bibliography

AAVV, *A Portrait of the Royal Ballet*, edited by Noel Goodwin, London: Michael O'Hara Books Ltd., 1988.

AAVV, *Le Kirov, Le Ballet de Leningrad, L'Ecole Vaganova,* "Ballet/Dance" in L'Avant-scène 8, Paris, February–March, 1982.

AAVV, *Rudolf Nureyev alla Scala,* edited by Vittoria Ottolenghi, Milan: Edizioni Teatro alla Scala, 2002.

Balanchine, George, *Complete Stories of the Great Ballets,* New York: Garden City: 1954.

Bailleux, Nathalie, and Remaury, Bruno, *Usi e costumi del vestire,* Trieste: Universale Electra/Gallimard, 1996.

Barnes, Clive, *Nureyev,* New York: Hélène Obolensky Enterprises, 1982.

Bettelheim, Bruno, *Il mondo incantato,* Milan: Universale Economica, Feltrinelli, 2002.

Bland, Alexander (Nigel Gosling and Maude Lloyd), *Fonteyn and Nureyev, La Storia di una coppia,* Rome: Di Giacomo Editore, 1978–81.

Bland, Alexander, *Observer of the Dance, 1958–1982,* London: Dance Books, 1985.

Bland, Alexander, *The Nureyev Image,* London: Studio Vista, 1976.

Bland, Alexander, *Valentino, ritratto di un film,* Milan: Sperling & Kupfler, 1977.

Bois, Mario, *Rudolf Noureev,* Paris, Editions Plume, 1993.

Bruhn, Erik, "Beyond Technique", in *Dance Perspectives,* no. 36, New York, 1968.

Capa, Robert, *Slightly Out of Focus,* Contrasto, 2002.

Devere, John, "In the Spotlight: Nureyev", in *Dilettante, the Renaissance Man, Magazine of the Arts, Entertainment & Eros,* New York, 1974.

Graham, Martha, *Blood Memory,* London and New York, 1991.

Haskell, Arnold L., *Balletomania, The Story of an Obsession,* London: Gollancz, 1934.

Haskell, Arnold L., *The National Ballet, A History and a Manifesto,* London: Adam & Charles Black, 1943.

Karsavina, Tamara, *Ballet Technique, A Series of Practical Essays,* New York: Theatre Arts Books, 1976.

Mann, Thomas, *La Morte a Venezia,* Rome: Gruppo Editoriale L'Espresso, 2002.

Nietzsche, Friedrich, *La nascita della tragedia,* Milan: Adelphi, 1979.

Nijinski, Romola (editor), *The Diary of Vaslav Nijinsky,* Berkeley and Los Angeles: University of California Press, 1968.

Pasi, Mario, and Pignotti, Luigi, *Nureyev, la sua storia e la sua vita,* Milan: Sperling & Kupfler, 1993.

Pastori, Jean-Pierre, *L'Homme et la Danse, Le Danseur du XVI au XX Siècle,* Fribourg: Office di Livre, 1980.

Percival, John, *Nureyev, Aspects of the Dancer,* London: Book Club Associates, 1976.

Quadri Franco, Bertoni Franco, Stearns Robert, *Robert Wilson,* Florence: Octavo, 1997.

Smakov, Gennady, *I grandi danzatori russi,* edited by Sergio Trombetta, Rome: Gremese Editore, 1987.

Solway, Diane, *Nureyev, His Life,* New York: William Morrow & Co. Inc., 1998.

Terry, Walter, *I Was There, Selected Dance Reviews and Articles 1973–1976,* New York: Audience Arts.

Trombetta, Sergio, *Rudolf Nureyev,* Milan: Casa Editrice Liber, 1993.

Vaganova, Agrippina, *Basic Principles of Classical Ballet, Russian Ballet Technique,* New York: Dover Publications, 1969 (translation into English: Anatole Chujoy).

Videography

An Evening with the Royal Ballet, London, BHE Production, 1963.

Cinderella, directed by Colin Nears, NVC Arts.

Dancing Through Darkness.

Don Quixote, directed by Rudolf Nureyev and Robert Helpmann, London, Dance Videos.

Fonteyn and Nureyev, The Perfect Partnership, written, directed, and produced by Peter Barry, 1985.

Giselle, London, Channel 5, 1986.

I Am a Dancer.

La Bayadère, directed by Alexandre Tarta, NVC Arts.

Romeo and Juliet, London, Channel 5, 1986.

Rudolf Nureyev. Ritratto, produced and directed by Patricia Foy, Antelope, Novara, De Agostini, 1992.

Ricordo di Rudolf Nureyev by Vittoria Ottolenghi, RAI Radiotelevisione Italiana, from "Maratona d'estate," 1993.

Videosera, Rai, 1978.